ADULT SOC

C000091507

Iain Ferguson and M

with responses from Bill Jordan, Mark Lymbery,
Dexter Whitfield, Ian Hood, Brian Smith and Claire Cairns

SERIES EDITORS:
Iain Ferguson and Michael Lavalette

This print edition first published in Great Britain in 2014 by

Policy Press
University of Bristol
6th Floor
Howard House
Queen's Avenue
Bristol BS8 1SD
UK
t: +44 (0)117 331 5020
f: +44 (0)117 331 5367
pp-info@bristol.ac.uk
www.policypress.co.uk

North American office:
Policy Press
c/o The University of Chicago Press
1427 East 60th Street
Chicago, IL 60637, USA
t: +1 773 702 7700
f: +1 773-702-9756
e:sales@press.uchicago.edu
www.press.uchicago.edu

© Policy Press 2014
Edition history: first published digitally in 2013

ISBN 978 1 44731 616 9 paperback

British Library Cataloguing in Publication Data
A catalogue record for this book is available from the British Library.

Library of Congress Cataloging-in-Publication Data
A catalog record for this book has been requested.

The right of Iain Ferguson and Michael Lavalette to be identified as authors of this work has been asserted by them in accordance with the Copyright, Designs and Patents Act 1988.

Cover design Policy Press
Printed in Great Britain by www.4edge.co.uk

OTHER TITLES AVAILABLE IN THIS SERIES

POVERTY AND INEQUALITY by Chris Jones and Tony Novak

PERSONALISATION by Peter Beresford

MENTAL HEALTH by Jeremy Weinstein

ETHICS by Sarah Banks

CHILDREN AND FAMILIES by Paul Michael Garrett

for more information about this series visit: www.policypress.co.uk/crdsw.asp

Policy Press also publishes the journal *Critical and Radical Social Work*; for more information visit: http://www.policypress.co.uk/journals_crsw.asp

Contents

Notes on contributors

Lead authors (and series editors)

Iain Ferguson is Professor of Social Work and Social Policy at the University of the West of Scotland and a member of the Steering Committee of the Social Work Action Network.

Michael Lavalette is Professor of Social Work and Social Policy at Liverpool Hope University and National Co-ordinator of the Social Work Action Network.

Respondents

Bill Jordan is Professor of Social Policy at the University of Plymouth. He is the author of many articles and books, including *Social work and social policy under austerity* (with Mark Drakeford) (Palgrave Macmillan, 2012).

Mark Lymbery is Associate Professor of Social Work at the University of Nottingham. He has written extensively on the implications of the personalisation agenda for social workers and service users.

Dexter Whitfield is Director of European Services Strategy Unit and is Adjunct Associate Professor, Australian Institute for Social Research, University of Adelaide. He is the author of *In place of austerity: Reconstructing the economy, state and public services* (Spokesman Books, 2012).

Ian Hood is co-ordinator of the Learning Disability Alliance Scotland.

Brian Smith is Branch Secretary of Glasgow UNISON and Convenor of Defend Glasgow Services.

Claire Cairns is Network Co-ordinator of the Coalition of Carers in Scotland.

Series editors' introduction

For much of its history, mainstream social work in Britain has been a fairly conservative profession. It has often reflected the dominant political ideologies of the day, while presenting itself as resolutely 'non-political'. Thus, the first social work organisation, the Charity Organisation Society (COS) (1869), rigorously adhered to the Poor Law notion that the poor could be divided into 'deserving' and 'undeserving', rejected any form of state intervention aimed at improving people's lives (including free school meals and old-age pensions) and saw the practice of individual casework as the best antidote to the spread of socialist ideas.

By contrast, social work in the 1960s reflected a broad social democratic consensus, evident in the recommendations of the Seebohm Report in England and Wales and the Kilbrandon Report in Scotland on the basis of which the new generic social work departments were established. In most respects, the social work of this period reflected a huge advance on the punitive individualism of the COS (and, it should be said, the punitive individualism of our own time). Even then, however, there was still a tendency to pathologise (albeit it was communities rather than individuals that were seen as failing) and to ignore the extent to which statutory social work intervention continued to be experienced by service users as oppressive and paternalistic. Be that as it may, the progressive possibilities of the new departments were soon cut short by the onset of a global economic crisis in 1973 to which the Labour governments of the time could offer no answer, except cuts and belt-tightening.

What is also true, however, as we have argued elsewhere (Lavalette and Ferguson, 2007), is that there has always been another tradition in social work, an activist/radical approach which has sought to present an alternative vision both to individualism and also to paternalist, top-down collectivism. This approach, which flourished in the UK in the 1970s, located the problems experienced by those who sought social work support in the material conditions of their lives and attempted to develop practice responses that challenged these conditions and their effects.

One source of theory underpinning that approach was the excellent series Critical Texts in Social Work and the Welfare State, edited by Peter Leonard and published by Macmillan.

Three decades on, this current series aims to similarly deepen and refresh the critical and radical social work tradition by providing a range of critical perspectives on key issues in contemporary social work. Social work has always been a contested profession but the need for a space for debate and discussion around ways forward for those committed to a social work practice informed by notions of social justice has never been greater. The issues are complex. How should social workers view personalisation, for example? In an era of austerity, can social work be about more than simply safeguarding and rationing scarce services? Will the integration of services in areas such as mental health lead to improved services or simply greater domination of medical models? Do social work practices offer an escape from managerialism and bureaucracy or are they simply a Trojan horse for privatisation?

These are some of the questions which contributors to this series – academics, practitioners, service users and movement activists – will address. Not all of those contributing to these texts would align themselves with the critical or radical tradition. What they have in common, however, is a commitment to a view of social work which is much wider than the currently dominant neoliberal models and a belief that notions of human rights and social justice should be at the heart of the social work project.

Adult social care: Iain Ferguson and Michael Lavalette

Adult social care in Britain has been at the centre of much media and public attention in recent years. Revelations of horrific abuse in learning disability settings, the collapse of major private care home providers, abject failures of inspection and regulation, and uncertainty over how the long-term care of older people should be funded have all given rise to serious public concern. Here, Iain Ferguson and

Michael Lavalette give an historical overview of adult social care and locate the roots of the current crisis in the undervaluing of older people and adults with disabilities and in the marketisation of social care over the past two decades. They examine recent developments in social work with adults, including the personalisation agenda, and critically examine the prospects for adult social care and social work in a context of seemingly never-ending austerity.

In the Responses section, a range of contributors including social work and social policy academics, representatives of voluntary organisations and trade union activists respond to the lead article. The book concludes with a reply to their comments by Iain Ferguson and Michael Lavalette.

The crisis in adult social care

Iain Ferguson and Michael Lavalette

Introduction

Two stories dominated the British news media in the early summer of 2011. The first concerned Winterbourne View, a private hospital for adults with learning disabilities near Bristol. Undercover filming for the BBC Panorama programme in late May 2011 showed staff there involved in appalling abuse of vulnerable residents, some of it verging on torture. Residents were seen being pinned down by staff members, slapped, dragged out of bed and, in one case, doused in water and left outside in cold weather. The programme caused public outrage and some weeks later, the home, owned by the private care company Castlebeck, was closed by the Department of Health and a group of eleven carers subsequently charged with some 45 counts alleging ill-treatment against or neglect of five victims.

Hard on the heels of the Winterbourne scandal came the announcement of the closure of Southern Cross, with 37,000 residents in over 750 care homes, the biggest provider of residential care for older people in the UK. The announcement caused huge anxiety among the residents of its care homes, their relatives and Southern Cross workers, 3,000 of whom lost their jobs. In echoes of the banking crisis of 2008, the state was forced to step in, with the Conservative–Liberal Democrat Coalition Government announcing that no resident

—

1

would be turned out onto the street. In the event, many of the homes were subsequently bought out by Four Seasons, the second largest care provider (the financial stability of which was also the subject of considerable speculation in the financial press during 2011: Bowers, 2012; Scourfield, 2012).

Any suggestion that Winterbourne and Southern Cross were simply 'bad apples', anomalies in an otherwise high-quality social care sector, was quickly dispelled by a second Panorama investigation in October of the same year. That programme gave examples of four former Winterbourne residents being assaulted in their *new* homes, the homes to which they had been moved.

More systematic evidence came in a Care Quality Commission Review of Learning Disability Services in 2012 (CQC, 2012). That report was based on unannounced visits to 145 establishments: 68 NHS Trusts providing assessment and secure services; 45 independent health-care services providing assessment and treatment; and 32 adult treatment and secure services. These establishments were inspected against compliance with two outcomes:

- care and welfare of people who use services;
- safeguarding people who use services from abuse.

The Review found that overall levels of compliance were low:

- Almost half of all locations – 48% – were non-compliant with care and welfare of people who use services and safeguarding people who use services from abuse.
- NHS locations were nearly twice as likely to be compliant with both of the outcomes compared to independent health care service providers (68% and 33% respectively).
- The majority of assessment and treatment services were compliant with both outcomes (51%).
- However, there were more people (58%) in the services that were non-compliant.

- Residents tended to stay for much longer in independent/private homes than in NHS facilities.
- A lack of person-centred planning was a significant feature.

What these crises highlight is the extent to which the care of vulnerable adults, whether older people or those with a mental or physical disability, is now often in the hands of individuals and companies whose primary concern is not with the welfare of their clients and residents but rather with the generation of profit. What they also show, however, as do similar crises in the NHS, such as the events at Mid-Staffordshire Hospital exposed in the Francis Report in early 2013 (Francis, 2013), is the abject failure of the regulatory mechanisms put in place by previous New Labour governments supposedly to ensure that such things could never happen. As the Panorama programme revealed, the General Care Council, the main regulator for England and Wales, had been informed by a whistleblower on more than one occasion of the abuse that was taking place at Winterbourne and at other Castlebeck homes. But the Commission had failed to act on the allegations. As part of the fall-out from the programme, the Chief Executive of the Commission, Cynthia Bower, was forced to announce her resignation less than a year later, with a House of Commons Public Accounts Committee expressing serious concerns about the organisation's 'governance, culture and leadership', including a culture of bullying against any staff members who spoke out (Public Accounts Committee, 2012).

However, while the examples referred to above represent the most visible face of the current crisis of social care in the UK, as we shall argue in this article, this is a crisis which touches on every aspect of care – residential, home care and day care – and affects every person who requires support for daily living. It is a crisis, we shall argue, whose roots lie in the conscious decision of Conservative governments in the late 1980s to open up social care provision to market forces. The rhetoric of 'choice' and the creation of a 'mixed economy of care' has been the smokescreen for a massive transfer of social care provision to the private sector, which means, for example, that whereas in the 1980s more than 90% of social care services were in local authority

–

3

hands, the bulk of social care provision is now controlled by huge companies such as Four Seasons, Serco and G4S (Gosling, 2008/2011). However, while this has been a crisis in the making for more than two decades, it has attained new and unforeseen depths since the election of a Conservative–Liberal Democrat Coalition Government in May 2010. The decision of that government to cut more than £80 billion of public sector spending in 2010, £18 billion of which will come from welfare spending, with further cuts of £2.6 billion to local authority spending in 2013, represents the biggest assault on the welfare state since its creation in 1948 and has brought the social care system to the brink of collapse (Yeates et al, 2010; Wintour and Stewart, 2013). The impact of these cuts was graphically spelled out in a letter to the *Observer* newspaper in 2012 by a coalition of 33 leading British charities including the British Red Cross, Mencap and the Royal National Institute for the Blind:

> The care system is in crisis. To deny this is woefully wrong. Without urgent reform, the social care system will fail the hundreds of thousands of people who rely on its services. Last week, Paul Burstow, the minister of state for care services, appeared before the health committee and told its members that 'there is no gap' in social care funding. We disagree. Every day, people tell us they are being let down by the care system – unable to access services, finding their care reduced and relying on family and friends to provide support. The government's figures show that this year, local authorities have spent 4.5% less in real terms on social care for older people alone than the previous year. Yet the demand for social care continues to rise. And with the number of disabled adults also increasing, in a climate of cuts more and more disabled people are unable to get the support they need to live their lives independently and be part of wider society. (*Observer*, 22 January 2012)

'Austerity' is now the universally recognised term for the draconian cuts in welfare spending imposed by governments across Europe at the behest of governing financial bodies such as the International Monetary Fund and the European Central Bank in response to the global economic crisis that erupted in 2008. It is a response whose primary concern is to shift the cost of paying for that crisis onto the shoulders of the working class and the poorest sections of society, despite the fact that, as even the former Governor of the Bank of England has acknowledged, they played no part in the creation of that crisis (Kirkup, 2011; Lapavitsas et al, 2012).

As the situation in Greece is already showing, the deepest cuts ever inflicted on welfare spending will create levels of misery not experienced since the Second World War (Garganas, 2012). Later in this article, we shall explore some of the ways in which the Coalition's cuts are now impacting on services in Britain. It would be wrong, however, to see the government's current programme of welfare retrenchment as simply being about cuts. In her book *The shock doctrine*, the writer and activist Naomi Klein explored the ways in which governments exploit the public's disorientation following massive collective shocks – wars, terrorist attacks, or natural disasters – to achieve control by imposing what she calls 'economic shock therapy' (Klein, 2008). In a much-cited example of Klein's thesis, soon after the financial crisis broke out in 2008, Rahm Emmanuel, an adviser to Barak Obama, argued in an interview that:

> You never want a serious crisis to go to waste. And what I mean by that is an opportunity to do things you think you could not do before. (Emmanuel, 2009)

Similarly, the sheer scale of the Coalition Government's assault on welfare indicates that what is involved here is something much more fundamental than simply 'deficit reduction' (Ferguson, 2011). Rather, it suggests that the Coalition Government in the UK is precisely seeking to use the current crisis to make structural and strategic advances that would be more difficult to push through in 'normal' times and which will change the whole basis of the post-war welfare settlement: in Kimber's words,

> To force the market even deeper into society, increase
> privatisation, weaken workers' collective strength, and make the
> welfare state serve capital rather than fulfill any of the needs of
> the majority. (Kimber, 2011)

The extent to which they can succeed in this aim, and how those of
us who wish to defend decent social care services should respond,
are questions to which we shall return in the final part of this article.

Before then, however, it is necessary to set the current crisis of care
in its wider historical and political context. To do that we shall look
first at the history of what is today termed 'adult social care' in the
UK and where this has sat within changes to welfare policy within
the development of capitalism in the UK. While there has never
been a 'golden age' of welfare, it is nevertheless true that struggles
from below (as well as reforms from above) have resulted in gains
for working people (the NHS being the most obvious example) that
need to be defended.

Secondly, we shall locate the roots of the current crisis in the market
fundamentalist (or neoliberal) policies initiated by the Conservative
governments of the 1980s, which for the most part were continued
by New Labour governments from 1997 onwards.

If many of the problems that the social care system is currently
experiencing stem from the neoliberal welfare policies of the past two
decades, it is also true that the cuts to welfare spending currently being
imposed by the Coalition Government have qualitatively deepened
the crisis and, in the next part of this article, we shall look at some
examples of how these cuts are destroying people's lives and services.

In the period immediately following the 2010 election, the idea of
the Big Society provided the overarching ideological framework for
the welfare policies of the Coalition. In response, some social work
commentators saw this idea as offering opportunities for the progressive
development of both social care and professional social work. While the
idea's emphasis on 'community' can indeed appear attractive after two
decades in which professional social work has been reduced to care
management, we shall suggest that within a wider context of austerity,

the progressive aspects of personalisation and community social work approaches have been subsumed by an agenda which preaches self-reliance and self-help to vulnerable individuals and resource-starved communities.

Finally, we shall look at alternatives. Much of the argument around social care has been framed in terms of what on what 'we as a country' can afford. The Dilnot Commission, for example, set up by the government in 2010 to make recommendations for 'a fair and sustainable funding system' for adult social care in England specifically ruled out funding social care out of general taxation on the grounds that it would be too expensive, offering instead a model of 'shared responsibility' (Dilnot Commission, 2011). Yet in its 2012 budget, the government felt able to reduce tax for the richest people in the country while its own figures showed that almost a thousand UK taxpayers earning more than £1m a year have a tax rate of less than 30% of their income, with the very richest often paying less than 10% and, according to HMRC, the 20 biggest 'legal' tax avoiders managing to reduce their income tax bills by a total of £145m in a year (BBC, 2012) . In contrast to Dilnot, therefore, we shall argue that there is no shortage of money to fund a social care system 'fit for purpose' in the 21st century; the question, rather, is one of political priorities.

So far, we have referred to social care 'in the UK'. Yet even within the UK, devolved governments in Scotland and in Wales have been able to develop policies which are less stridently market-oriented (albeit within an approach which remains broadly neoliberal). In Scotland, for example, personal care is available without charge for everyone aged 65 and over who has been assessed by the local authority as needing it. In addition, several of the key 'reforms' being implemented by the Westminster government such as the Health and Social Care Act 2012 and the Public Services (Social Value) Act 2012 will not apply north of the border (Mooney and Scott, 2012). To say this is not to paint what is in practice a mildly social-democratic Scottish National Party government as more radical than it is: the reason that that government wishes greater fiscal powers, for example, is to allow it to make Scottish capitalism more 'competitive' by reducing taxes for large multinational companies! Rather, it is to argue that governments can make political choices about how to respond to a global crisis. What choices they do make, of course, in the area of social care as elsewhere, will depend in large part on the influence that a range of social forces bring to bear on them. In the final part of the article, we shall consider the kind of alliances that will be necessary not only to defend existing services from further cuts and austerity but also to construct a more democratic and inclusive system of social care built around people's needs and not the generation of profit.

Capitalism and adult social care

> Capital ... takes no account of the health and the length of life of the worker, unless society forces it to do so. Its answer to the outcry about the physical and mental degradation, the premature death, the torture of over-work, is this: Should that pain trouble us, since it increases our pleasure (profit)? (Marx, 1867/1976, p 381)

Capitalism is a system that faces many – often competing and contradictory – demands. In *Capital,* Marx (1867) exposed the brutality of the capitalist mode of production in its treatment of those who are forced to sell their labour power – and, equally significantly, the barbaric abandonment of those who, for whatever reason, are unable to engage in paid employment.

The requirement of any particular unit of capital is for docile, cheap flexible labour, working long hours and with few barriers in the way of profit maximisation. But capitalism is a system of 'many competing capitals' and, as a whole, it has certain systemic needs that have to be fulfilled if it is to flourish. Thus one of the things that capitalism, as a system, requires is the need to reproduce labour on a daily, intergenerational and social basis. The system requires workers to have enough food, sleep, and so on, to be able to function the following day; to be adequately trained and educated (which may require longer-term investment); it needs future generations of workers (and thus

–

there needs to be some place or space for growing children) and it needs workers to be socialised into the main tenets of the system (to accept the inevitability of wage labour, for example). All of this can be problematic and all can be contested (especially by organised labour who, individually and collectively, may have alternative visions about how their needs can and should be met).

Ensuring labour reproduction within capitalism is problematic for individuals, families and the system as a whole. It is particularly problematic with regard to the 'non-working' population (children, the unemployed, those with special needs, the disabled, the elderly). How can or should they be supported?

In the post-Second World War era, the central way this was managed in Europe was via some form of welfare state. As Ian Gough (1979) put it: 'the use of state power to modify the reproduction of labour power and to maintain the non-working population' (pp 44–5). Most state investment in welfare services has a 'dual character'. On the one hand it brings benefit to the recipient(s) whilst, at the same time, it is an investment in future economic assets. Thus education, the NHS or benefit payments bring important immediate support services to users, whilst, at the same time, help to reproduce or maintain a healthy, trained or educated future working population.

But, in his important study *Capitalism and the construction of old age*, Phillipson (1982) suggests that, whilst most social investment contains this 'dual character' this is not the case with expenditure on the elderly and those with a range of physical and learning disabilities. Investment in older people has no positive future 'investment function' and, indeed, may actually help keep people alive longer (hardly a 'problem' most of us might think!), consuming resources without producing any economic return for the system. Borsay (2003) argues that, since 1750, disabled people have been marginalised within the labour market, viewed as a drain on scarce resources and 'excluded' within society as a whole; whilst Thomson (1998) makes similar points regarding the history of state policy with regard to those with learning disabilities. The domination of the 'medical model', which perceived disability as a 'personal trouble' and a 'medical condition' to be cured, influenced policy initiatives, shaped by notions of 'control', segregation, institutionalisation and eugenics.

It is these features that partly explain why adult social care services have always been the 'Cinderella' social service. So how has capitalism dealt with the 'problem' of non-working old age and disabled populations?

From the Industrial Revolution onwards, through the 19th and early 20th centuries, state policy towards 'the poor' – the vast majority of whom were 'working poor' – was shaped by the philosophies of laissez-faire and 'less eligibility'. Within the dominant philosophies, the poor were expected to be 'self-reliant' and support themselves and their families at all times and in all circumstances; failure to be self-reliant equated to moral failure. Thus the purpose of state policy – most notoriously, in England and Wales, in the form of the Poor Law Amendment Act 1834[1] – was to 'remoralise' the poor, to enforce self-sufficiency and to promote commitment to the 'virtues' of work. These were part of what Engels (1845) described as 'the most open declaration of war by the bourgeoisie upon the proletariat'.

Of course in capitalist economies unemployment and under-employment are not questions of individual morality, but are determined by the vagaries of the market. When economies slump, industries, factories and offices close and workers are thrown onto the scrap heap. Further, 'unless', as Marx put it, 'capital is forced by society' to do otherwise, this is a system that abandons the old, the vulnerable and those with a range of disabilities, leaving them isolated and struggling in desperate poverty.

In the second half of the 19th century the principle of less eligibility was enforced through the workhouse test. From 1834 outdoor relief was to cease (at least in theory, if not always in practice) and those who failed to be self-reliant had to throw themselves on the mercy of the workhouse. The workhouse regime was deliberately brutal. It aimed to act as a deterrent.

> The regulation of ... [the] workhouses, or as the people call
> them, Poor Law Bastilles, is such as to frighten away everyone

who has the slightest prospect of life without this form of public charity. The workhouse has been made the most repulsive residence which the ingenuity of a follower of Malthus can invent. (Engels, 1845)

For working-class families and communities the desperation created by enforced unemployment and underemployment created the social and material conditions for the 're-establishment of the working-class family', which in some parts of the country had been breaking down under the pressures of generalised proletarianisation (Humphries, 1977a, 1977b; German, 1989). Working-class family and kinship networks became the only reliable source of mutual support for children, elderly relatives and family members with a range of disabilities. It led to campaigns (albeit largely unsuccessful) for a 'family wage' (earned by working men but large enough to support an entire family) and, in the process, reinforced the sexual division of labour and women's oppression as they became identified as the main carers within the home and family. What is, today, called 'informal care' has always meant unpaid care provided, overwhelmingly, by women family members within the home.

But where family support was not available people had to turn to the workhouse.

Parliamentary returns from 1861 and 1871 suggest that the workhouse was made up of two types of population. The first was a more transient body of young people who entered the workhouse for a relatively short period in the face of acute crisis and who left whenever they were able and jobs became available (often moving in and out of the workhouse throughout their adult life). But there was also a 'semi-permanent' population, those who lived in the workhouse for up to five years or more.

Most long-term residents were admitted because they were old and infirm or young and dependent. The workhouse provided a home for the aged, the decrepit and the geriatric and a hospital for those who were temporarily or chronically sick.

—
11

These, the non-able bodied, accounted for up to one half of all paupers during the nineteenth century. Extended care within the workhouse also arose from disability and mental illness. The proportion of pauper lunatics [*sic*] rose dramatically in the second half of the nineteenth century. In 1842 one in one hundred paupers was classed as insane but by 1910 the proportion had risen to one in every eight paupers (Englander, 1998, p 34)

The Poor Law system, as envisaged by Chadwick in 1832, attempted to classify and separate different groups of 'paupers'. Chadwick railed against the 'mixed workhouse'. Instead he argued for separate institutions for 'the impotent' (that is the elderly and the infirm), children, 'lunatics' and the 'able-bodied' (who would be separated by sex). It was not until 1870 that Poor Law Guardians were instructed to organise inmate populations by the cause of their poverty and by their 'character'. There was little central funding for this project, but gradually separate buildings started to appear: workhouse hospitals often provided free medical assistance for local communities, and vaccinations and isolation to stop the spread of contagious disease; asylum institutions, under the auspices of Asylum Boards, provided institutional accommodation for people with learning disabilities; pauper children started to attend 'Barrack' schools and there were significant changes to how the elderly were treated within the workhouse institutions (with a relaxation in the rules governing their dress codes and dietary needs). By the late 19th century, therefore, there was a different orientation within much state policy, marked by what is often termed 'liberal collectivism' or a more interventionist state.

The 'seedbed' of the post-war welfare state was put in place in the last decades of the 19th century and the first decade of the 20th. The old certainties of 'laissez-faire' were thrown into question as a result of Britain's declining relative economic performance (Hobsbawm, 1987); by the threat to Empire presaged by the Boer Wars; by the discovery of poverty and social problems among the 'outcast' populations of Britain's towns and cities (Stedman-Jones, 1971) – which, in the case of ill health and disease, for example, often spread beyond poor

—

communities to threaten the city-dwelling middle classes; and by the growth of militant working-class collective action within the 'second wave of unionism' and the mass strike wave of the late 1880s (Charlton, 2000). In this context a more interventionist state began to develop to try and manage some of the social problems created by 'naked' market capitalism (Langan and Schwarz, 1985). But the competing pressures meant that the developing state welfare system embodied different, often contradictory, motivations.

Thus one of the 'solutions' to deal with the ageing population and the care of older people was agitation for an adequate pensions system. Most mainstream history books (eg Jones, 2000) suggest that the Old Age Pensions Act 1908 was guided through Parliament and onto the statute books by Lloyd George; however, the reality is somewhat different.

Pensions were first raised within the political process at the election of 1885 – partly a reflection of the growing numbers of working-class voters, which was itself the result of the Reform Act 1867. But, as with much within the parliamentary system, little concrete happened. A Royal Commission on the Aged Poor in 1895 looked at the 'possibility' of creating a pensions system and estimated that there were two million people aged 65 or over and two-thirds were in want. These numbers, they argued, made it quite clear that the 'disadvantages' of a pension system (that is, its costs) far outweighed any benefits.

But the pensions movement did not disappear. In 1899, in Newcastle, representatives from trade union branches, the co-operative movement and the Trades Council network gathered to demand action. In the next few months there were similar conferences in Leeds, Bradford, Manchester, Bristol, Birmingham, Glasgow and London (Goodman, 1998). The result was the creation of the National Pensions Committee, which was to campaign for retirement at age 65 and a flat-rate pension payable to men and women. It was this popular agitation that brought the pension issue to the fore.

The agitation eventually led to the passing of the Old Age Pensions Act 1908: a significant landmark in British social policy. Nevertheless, payment was restricted to 'non-aliens', over the age of 70, and included a number of tests to ensure it was only paid to the 'deserving'. Further, the level at which the pension was paid was not enough to support someone completely – it was not intended to encourage 'retirement' (although retirement to a life of relative leisure in old age expanded throughout the 20th century for those at the upper end of the income distribution). Claimants would have to rely on savings (or a private pension) if they wished to retire; the majority had to supplement their pension with work. Thus the legislation was, at best, a wage supplement that maintained working-class older people as a partial labour reserve within the economy.

As a result, Phillipson notes that, during the first half of the 20th century: 'old age, while moving some to the workhouse, moved others to the sea [to the 'retirement towns' on the south coast, for example], leaving ... for the majority in between the weary monotony enforced by life around the poverty line' (1982, p 21). This bleak picture continued during the inter-war period. Despite the spread of pension cover, the 'hungry thirties' afforded fewer opportunities for older people to work. It also placed greater strains on extended family support networks, many of whom put up with untold hardship to avoid the indignity and detailed scrutiny imposed by 'relief officers' from the Public Assistance Committees. It was not until the post-war 'Beveridge reforms' were implemented, combined with the expansion of final salary pension schemes during the economic boom conditions of the post-war period, that many working-class working people could look forward to retirement at 60/65 without, for many, the necessity of work in retirement or the threat of workhouse-like institutions.

Despite its inadequacies the pension was won via collective working-class pressure. But the 'interventionist state' was not a benevolent or humane beast. The increasing separation of older people, disabled people and those with learning disabilities into state institutions in the first half of the 20th century was shaped by a variety of ideologies including eugenics (with Winston Churchill among those who advocated castration of the 'mentally enfeebled' while he was Home Secretary in 1910–11 [Gilbert, 2009]) and a social paternalism.

For those with a range of learning disabilities the Mental Deficiency Act 1913 was a draconian piece of legislation that classified categories of 'deficiency'. The legislation delineates between 'mental defectives' (who could be incarcerated for life and whose symptoms had to be present from birth or early life), 'idiots' (who were 'so deeply defective in mind as to be unable to guard against common physical dangers'), 'imbeciles' (who were 'incapable of managing themselves or their affairs'), the 'feeble-minded' (whose condition was 'so pronounced that they require care, supervision and control for their own protection or the protection of others') and 'moral defectives' (people who, from an early age, displayed 'some permanent mental defect coupled with strong vicious or criminal propensities on which punishment had little or no effect'). Such classification allowed the incarceration of numerous people in large asylums and became the policy choice of successive governments until it was repealed in 1959. The classification of 'moral defectives' was used to incarcerate a range of people who were deemed to have breached the moral order in some form – including, on occasion, unmarried mothers.

The incarceration of large numbers of people in a range of brutalising institutions meant that by the 1960s there was a growing critique of such 'asylums' (Goffman, 1961). The post-war boom conditions in the economy, the increasing demands for labour, the expansion of the welfare state and, within the new social movements, demands that the welfare on offer should be 'humanised' and reflect the needs of different sections of the community in different ways all put pressure on the existing system of adult social care.

The pressure grew to develop more community-based means of adult support – in terms of support both for those who remained within the family home and for those who required some form of looked-after care in smaller units within their communities. And it was by exploiting such critiques and moving policy in the direction of 'care in the community' that the Conservative governments of the 1980s were able to introduce significant marketisation into the system.

Of course, in the field of adult social care government policy has shifted over the decades, but there are some remarkable continuities in

15

terms of government drivers. The old poor law ideas of the morality of 'self-reliance' and of self-support have always been present. Where care is required, the first port of call has always been, where possible, the unpaid care provided by the family (and overwhelmingly women within the home). Those who need support – whether people with disabilities or the older population – always face pressure to combine care, support or pensions with cheap paid labour when the economy requires them and they are often amongst the first to be expelled when the economy enters recession.

The inequalities of modern capitalism are reified among those who access adult social care. Health, longevity and disability are all deeply affected by our unequal, class-divided society. And of course this means that – like all social work practice – adult social work is overwhelmingly concerned with work with working-class people in need. But in the field of social work, the adult services have always been marginalised and stigmatised. Too often, in place of adult social work, what has been on offer is a cheap, devalued 'adult social care'.

These continuities have continued as welfare services have increasingly been reshaped within the marketisation of welfare that has occurred over the last 25 years.

The marketisation of social care

> His favourite council was said to be one in mid-West America which employed almost no one and met just once a year to award all contracts to the private sector. (Timmins on Nicholas Ridley, Margaret Thatcher's Secretary of State for the Environment: Timmins, 1996, p 474)

The Conservative Government that came to power in 1979 was one of the most consciously ideological in British history. It was elected in the wake of a 'winter of discontent' in which millions of low-paid workers had struggled against a Labour government presiding over the biggest fall in living standards since the Second World War. The new government under Margaret Thatcher sought a different solution to the problems of British capitalism to that of its predecessors, both Labour and Conservative. In place of the state interventionist strategies that had characterised post-war politics, Thatcher saw the radical extension of market forces – and the removal of all barriers to the free operation of these forces – as the only way to address long-term problems of profitability exposed by the oil crisis of 1973 (Harvey, 2005).

Within that political and economic project, the future development of the welfare state initially had a low priority, for two reasons. First, as the British Social Attitudes Surveys published since 1983 have consistently demonstrated, the welfare state is extremely popular with the British public, for reasons discussed in the previous section. Any moves by the government to increase market involvement in the welfare state immediately following its election would undoubtedly have met with considerable resistance. That aside, as Timmins notes, the government had a more immediate priority (Timmins, 1996, p 372). Following a high level of industrial struggle over the previous decade, the British trade union movement was seen by the Conservatives as being the main barrier to raising profit levels in the UK and its weakening or destruction, therefore, their central task. Their strategy for achieving that goal had been developed prior to the 1979 election by Nicholas Ridley, one of Margaret Thatcher's closest political allies. The Ridley Plan, as it was known, sought to learn from the mistakes of the previous Conservative Government of 1970–74 and his strategy involved taking on the unions one at a time, retreating when judged tactically necessary, and postponing a fight with the most powerful section of the working class – the miners – until the time was right. With hindsight, it proved to be a very effective strategy, due in large part to the unwillingness of the leadership of the Labour Party and the Trade Union Congress to throw their full weight behind workers' struggles, notably that of the miners during their year-long strike in 1984–85 (Callinicos and Simons, 1985; Seymour, 2011).

A consequence of these priorities was that it was not until 1987, following the election of a third Conservative government, that serious consideration was given as to how to increase market involvement in the welfare state. Here again, Ridley was to play an important role. In what was to prove a highly influential pamphlet, *The local right*, Ridley argued that the role of local councils should be 'enabling, not providing' (Ridley, 1988): councils, in other words, should stimulate, facilitate and monitor services but services which could be purchased from the private sector and need not be provided by the councils themselves.

It was a view which was enshrined in the Griffiths Report on community care later in the same year, which laid the basis for the NHS and Community Care Act 1990. According to its author, Sainsbury's Managing Director Sir Roy Griffiths:

> This is a key statement. The role of the public sector is essentially to ensure that care is provided. How it is provided is an important but secondary consideration and local authorities must show they are getting and providing real value. (Griffiths, 1988)

As Harris has argued, behind this seemingly non-ideological approach, the 1990 Act provided the essential framework for the creation of a market in social care, through enshrining in law a purchaser/provider split and actively promoting the role of the 'independent' sector (Harris, 2003).

The speed and extent of marketisation since then has been astonishing. In the 1980s, 90% of local-authority commissioned care services were provided by the public sector. Today, the majority – residential care, day care and home care – are provided by the private sector. As Gosling has suggested, the privatisation of social care services is arguably the most extensive outsourcing of a public service yet undertaken in the UK (Gosling, 2008/2011, p 8). It is a transformation that began under the Conservatives in the early 1990s but one that continued under subsequent New Labour governments, whose similarly 'non-ideological' approach to social policy, based on the rhetoric of 'modernisation' and 'what works', also concealed a commitment to the role of the market in social care scarcely less fervent than that of their supposed political opponents (Harris and White, 2009).

The justification for the introduction of market forces to social care was twofold. First, it was argued, opening up social care to private providers would increase choice, since in place of the 'one-size-fits-all' model that (allegedly) characterised local-authority provided services through most of the post-war period, service users would now be able to shop around and choose whichever service best fitted their needs. Second, the introduction of competition would improve the quality of care since customers would clearly choose to purchase those services which best met their needs while those that failed to do so would go out of business.

A series of studies and reports highlight just how different the reality has proved to be. The following were among the key findings of a major report commissioned by UNISON into the rise of the 'public services industry':

- 'Marketisation' has created a multi-billion pound 'industry', generating massive profits for a narrow group of giant companies.
- Key players in the 'public services industry' have been banks, infrastructure funds, private equity houses, consultancy firms, multinational corporations, 'third sector' enterprises, and a new breed of 'multi-service' firms focused on winning government contracts.
- Private sector providers – including many operated by private equity houses focused on short-term financial returns – now dominate much of the social care 'market place'.
- Private equity investors have had a core role in transferring public sector assets into commercial activities.
- Downturns in demand, along with the government's austerity programme, have brought some privatised providers of key public services to the edge of collapse.
- Private equity tends to be a short-term holder of assets, seeking fast returns on investments. This encourages sometimes repeated transfers of ownership, undermining service continuity.
- While some companies have been very successful, others have been failures.

- Public bodies then have to pick up the pieces and meet the additional costs (Gosling, 2008/2011).

Far from increasing choice and control, then, the introduction of competition into residential social care has resulted in the domination of the market by a small number of very powerful multinational corporations (including, for example, the Royal Bank of Scotland and the Qatar Investment Fund) whose primary concern is not the welfare of the residents in the homes that they own but rather with maximising their profits. When they fail to do so sufficiently or where there are larger profits to be made elsewhere, then they will simply pull out, creating massive instability in the sector and undermining the continuity of care, which is such an essential element of good-quality social care.

Nor has the increased role of the private sector in social care resulted in improved quality of care. An investigation by the *Financial Times* in 2011 showed that the quality of care in one in seven privately run homes in England was rated 'poor' or 'adequate' by the government regulator. The low ratings indicate potentially serious problems such as a failure adequately to feed or clean residents. By contrast, the low ratings applied to only one in eleven homes run by non-profit organisations or local authorities. The report cited an inspector from the regulatory body, the Care Quality Commission, who wished to remain anonymous, as saying: "Fundamentally, it's now got to a point of being dangerous [for residents] – and it's going to get worse. If I had a relative who needed to go to a care service, I'd be concerned" (O'Connor and O'Murchu, 2011).

An inquiry carried out by the Equality and Human Rights Commission into the human rights of older people receiving home care expressed similar concerns. While around half of the older people, friends and family members who gave evidence to the inquiry expressed satisfaction with their care, the inquiry also revealed many examples of older people's human rights being breached, including physical or financial abuse, disregarding their privacy and dignity, failing to support them with eating or drinking, treating them as if they were invisible, and paying little attention to what they want. Some were surprised that they had any choice at all as they thought they had little say in how their care was arranged (EHRC, 2011). In its conclusions the Commission identified five main factors contributing to the poor quality of care received by older people living at home. These were:

- the impact of age discrimination;
- a lack of informed choice about home care;
- a lack of investment in care workers;
- output-driven commissioning; and
- the climate of financial constraints.

Some of the roots of age discrimination were discussed earlier, while in principle it should not be impossible to provide older people with information about the choices open to them (although independent advocacy services would undoubtedly help). However, the remaining factors relate directly to the marketisation of social care discussed above. While historically social care workers have always experienced poor conditions and low rates of pay, the introduction of competition over the past 20 years into social care has led to a 'race to the bottom' (Cunningham, 2008) in which staff pay, conditions and training have undoubtedly deteriorated, with the *Financial Times* investigation showing that the private sector pays lower wages on average than the non-profit and public sectors and has higher staff turnover rates (O'Connor and O'Murchu, 2011).

These same pressures of competition also apply to commissioning, where, despite lip-service being paid to issues of quality, ultimately it is price that trumps all other considerations.

One aspect of this – and a theme which recurs throughout the EHRC Report – is the very limited amount of time that carers are permitted to spend with their clients. The report cites one example from the daughter of an older woman with Huntington's disease, who described the serious consequences of her mother receiving no help with eating or drinking (treatment, which the report's authors argue, might well amount to inhuman and degrading treatment within Article 3 of the European Convention on Human Rights):

> Carers were supposed to feed and give drinks but simply left them beside a person who was physically unable to feed herself because the carers had to go to their next client. My mother went down to 7 stone. Someone with Huntington's needs an hour per meal to swallow food/drink, and special care when it all falls out of their mouth, and they get very damp and dirty. They also need 4,000 calories per day to maintain body weight due to the chorea movements that constantly burn energy" (Daughter of older woman, South of England, in EHRC, 2011, p 45).

Nor was this an issue of uncaring workers. The report quotes several workers who shared their clients' frustration at the lack of time they were permitted to carry out their caring tasks. For one:

> "The least satisfying is not having enough time, you try not to hurry them [older people] (or to let them know you haven't enough time) but you are aware that your next client is watching the clock and waiting for you to arrive" (Home care worker – voluntary sector provider, South West, in EHRC, 2011, p 72).

As the report's authors note, their evidence suggests that it may be difficult for providers to adopt a human rights-based approach to home care unless the problem of time constraints can be addressed (EHRC, 2011, p 61).

From Big Society to austerity

'Doing more for less' has been a key tenet of the managerialist approaches that have transformed social work and social care over the past two decades (Ferguson, 2008; Harris and White, 2009). Well before the onset of a global economic crisis in 2008, the growing pressure on social workers and social care workers to achieve more with fewer resources was well documented. For one respondent in Jones' much-cited study of front-line social work, for example:

> I now work much harder than I have ever worked in my life. You are expected to work at a much faster rate with no breaks. It is no wonder that so many social workers are off with stress and on long-term sick. It is appalling and it is going to get worse now that we have all these league tables that are beginning to drive things (cited in Jones, 2005, p 101).

Nevertheless, the cuts to welfare spending imposed by the Coalition Government in 2010 marked a qualitative shift – were 'historic' according to one influential analysis (Yeates et al, 2010). The Coalition's Comprehensive Spending Review in October of that year saw the deepest cuts to public spending – £80 billion, £18 billion of which from welfare spending – since the creation of the welfare state. A further £11.5 billion was cut from public spending in the Chancellor's Comprehensive Spending Review of June 2013, much of it falling on welfare spending (Wintour and Stewart, 2013).

These cuts affect the poorest sections of the community in two ways. First, reflecting a demonising agenda which has resonances with the 'less eligibility' philosophy of the Poor Law discussed above, they involve reductions in benefits which seem primarily designed to make life on benefits so unpleasant that people will take any job whatsoever, regardless of whether jobs actually exist and despite the evidence of the Joseph Rowntree Foundation that people working but receiving benefits – the 'in-work poor' – now outnumber those who are out of work and receiving benefits (Aldridge et al, 2012). Other than private moneylenders, it is difficult to see who can gain from requiring people who become unemployed to wait a full week before they receive any benefits, while in the absence of a sufficient supply of one-bedroom houses, a bedroom tax which requires those with 'too many rooms' to move out of their social housing often into private rented accommodation will only benefit private landlords and will actually increase spending on housing benefit. It is difficult, therefore, to resist the conclusion that these 'reforms' are driven by ideology and politics rather than economics.

Second, cuts of around one third to local authority spending between 2010 and 2013 have meant closure of local authority services, cuts to the grants of voluntary organisations and rising eligibility criteria. What that has meant in practice was shown in a survey of more than 30 local authorities in England in April 2012 conducted by *The Independent* newspaper (Morris, 2012). The survey found that, against a background of growing demand on services, these authorities were on average planning to reducing spending in that year by 3 per cent. To do so, they were employing a range of strategies including the closure of council facilities such as care homes and day centres, greater use of 'reablement' (intensive short-term input of resources after someone has been discharged from hospital), raising eligibility criteria and increasing charges. By 2011, for example, 120 councils, or around 80%, had set their eligibility level at substantial or critical levels. In practice, this means that those deemed to have moderate or low eligibility will be left to depend on family, friends or their own resources (although a number of successful legal challenges may limit councils' capacity to ration services in this way).

In June 2013, the government also signalled that its planned national eligibility threshold for adult social care – set to come into force in April 2015 through the current Care Bill – would be equivalent to the current 'substantial' threshold used by the vast majority of councils – a huge blow to older people's and disability charities who have campaigned strongly for a 'moderate' threshold (Community Care, 2013a).

Other strategies referred to in the survey included increased use of telecare to reduce personal care and also increased outsourcing of council services.

These cuts, alongside the wholesale privatisation of health and social care services, form two of the three planks of the Coalition Government's 2010 strategy for welfare reform. The third was the Big Society.

Social work and the Big Society

When first mooted by the then Opposition leader David Cameron (Cameron, 2009), there were three broad responses to the Big Society idea: first, widespread scepticism, a suspicion that the idea was little more than warm words that lacked any real substance; secondly, a view that the Big Society was no more than a cover for cuts (Toynbee, 2010; Holman, 2011); thirdly, a more sympathetic response that saw Cameron's idea as an attempt to address genuine issues of community breakdown, low levels of happiness and well-being in British society. Interestingly, among those who were prepared to engage with the idea in this third way were some leading social work academics not normally sympathetic to Conservative policies, notably Bill Jordan (Jordan, 2011). For Jordan, the Big Society idea was above all a response to New Labour's managerial approach to social work and one that provides the profession with an opportunity to reconnect with a moral (as opposed to a technocratic) agenda. The rationale for the Big Society, he suggested, was twofold:

On the one hand, it offers to deliver citizens from the technocratic formalism of the new public services, with their obsessions about rules, systems and checklists; it invites participation, enthusiasm and commitment. On the other, it promises to restore to professionals the power to exercise judgement, critique and expertise – to take back decision-making from the government, managers and inspectors (Jordan, 2011, p 3).

More fundamentally, Jordan suggested, the Big Society posed the question of what social services were really about. New Labour reduced everything to a network of incentives and contracts that sought to steer people's behaviour, without engaging them morally. By contrast, he suggested:

The Big Society is an attempt to reinstate moral (in place of contractual) regulation, in at least part of this field (Jordan, 2011, p 4).

While, however, the critique of New Labour's technocratic ethos was one element of the Big Society discourse, it was wrong to see it as the main element. Rather, as his 2009 lecture shows, Cameron's primary concern was with the relationship between individuals and the state and, above all, with the alleged role of that state in creating dependency and undermining responsibility. His was, however, a rather selective view of dependency and responsibility. He made no reference, for example, to those highly paid bankers whose reckless and irresponsible behaviour contributed to the creation of a global economic crisis in 2008, resulting in their having to be bailed out by that same 'Big State' (Mason, 2009). Rather, Cameron's concern was with those at opposite end of society who, whether through age, disability or unemployment, rely to a greater or lesser degree on the welfare state. In that sense, the Big Society was a continuation of, and response to, his earlier thesis that Britain was a 'Broken Society', broken not by the monetarist policies of 1980s Conservative governments that closed whole swathes of industry, destroying working-class communities and leaving millions unemployed and without hope (Davies, 1998), but rather by the alleged fecklessness of the poor and their inability to break out of dependence on welfare. Far from the Big Society idea representing a break with, or rejection of, this worldview, it is more accurately seen as a development of it, as an attempt to weaken and undermine the popular expectation that citizens can look to the welfare state for support when they are sick, unemployed or elderly, and instead to shift responsibility from state to individual. As Coote has rightly argued:

Beneath its seductive language about giving more power to citizens, the 'Big Society' is a major programme of structural change that aims to overturn the post-war welfare state. The key idea is to divest the state of responsibility for meeting needs and managing risks that individuals cannot cope with alone.

—

Functions that have been funded through taxes and carried out by publicly owned bodies for more than sixty years are to be transferred to 'civil society' and exercised through self-help, mutual aid, charity, philanthropy, local enterprise and big business (Coote, 2011, p 82).

With hindsight, the idea of the Big Society is perhaps best seen as part of the attempt by the leadership of the Conservative Party pre-2010 to break with its image as the 'nasty' party and with the brutal individualism of the Thatcher years. Three years on, with no end in sight to the global crisis or to the austerity policies with which most Western governments have responded to that crisis, it is perhaps not surprising that the rhetoric of the Big Society has all but vanished, to be replaced once more by a stigmatising 'strivers vs shirkers' rhetoric that echoes and surpasses the demonisation of those on benefits which characterised the Conservative governments of the 1980s.

Personalisation, empowering communities and social action

While the Big Society thesis has proved to be even more ephemeral than its critics imagined, some of the ideas associated with it may prove to be more long-lasting. Here, three of these will be touched on: personalisation; empowering communities and encouraging social action; and opening up public services.

Personalisation: empowering service users or transferring risk?

Personalisation (or Self-Directed Support, as it is known in Scotland) refers to the policy of providing individuals with a sum of money (known as a direct payment or an individual/personal budget) to allow them to purchase their own care on the market. While it is an approach initially pioneered by disability activists in the Independent Living Movement in the 1980s and 1990s as a means of escaping paternalist services (Campbell and Oliver, 1996; Slorach, 2011), the fact that it is also compatible with a neoliberal consumerism that constructs service users as rational customers has made it popular with both Conservative and New Labour governments since the mid-1990s (Ferguson, 2007). In an example of the policy continuity noted earlier in this article, personalisation is now promoted by the Coalition as a key element of the Big Society agenda, since it involves shifting responsibility from the state to the individual service user (DH, 2010a).

Increased choice and control is offered as the rationale for the shift towards personalisation and self-directed support. Yet in a context of huge cuts to local authority budgets, in some cases personalisation is resulting in *less* choice as service users find themselves unable to afford the costs not only of new providers but also of their existing local authority-provided services (where these continue to survive). A scrutiny report of Glasgow City Council in 2011 by the main inspection agency in Scotland found that while senior managers were upbeat about the shift to self-directed support, by contrast:

> Almost all carers, staff, providers and partner agencies we met were discontented – to varying degrees – with the level and nature of communication with the service. They were also concerned about the process, the speed of change and the reductions in many care packages. Many of those involved perceived the local authority's motive as primarily or solely that of saving money rather than that of improving services (SCSWIS, 2011, p 9).

Given that Glasgow City Council had explicitly sought to make savings of 20% in the social care budget in the move towards personalisation, there are clearly grounds for such concerns.

From a worker perspective, personalisation has been promoted both north and south of the border as offering a new philosophy for social work. The reality, however, is proving to be rather different. A study conducted by researchers at the University of Strathclyde, for example, found that a major concern of the social care workers whom they interviewed related to the context of austerity in which personalisation is being implemented and the suspicion that the progressive rhetoric of choice and control associated with the policy is being used as a cover for cuts (Cunningham and Nickson, 2011).

More recently, an annual personalisation survey for *Community Care* magazine in association with UNISON found in 2013 that adult social workers were becoming more doubtful that the personalisation agenda would deliver for service users or themselves, with 66% stating that the introduction of personalisation two years previously had increased, not lessened bureaucracy There was also concern among these workers that impending cuts in councils' budgets could cause personalisation to stagnate (*Community Care*, 2013b).

Empowering communities?

A second strand of the Big Society project involved 'giving local councils and neighbourhoods more power to take decisions and shape their area'. On the one hand, that involved the apparent rediscovery of community development, reflected, for example, in the proposal to employ 5,000 community organisers in England (Conservative Party, 2010). This emphasis on community was initially welcomed by some commentators who saw it as providing social workers with an opportunity to move away from the narrow, individualised care management approaches that have dominated British social work for the past two decades and to reconnect with a community social work approach that has all but disappeared from contemporary education and practice (Beresford, 2010). While in principle opportunities to reconnect with more collective approaches should be welcomed, here too, as with personalisation, it is impossible to ignore the context of austerity in which such initiatives are being promoted. Many charities and voluntary organisations (including youth services), seen by the government as the backbone of the Big Society project, depend heavily on local authority funding and have been among the main victims of these cuts (Kane and Allen, 2011). Given that weakening of community capacity, it is difficult to see how community development in this context can take anything but the most highly conservative form, aimed at getting the poorest communities to pull themselves up by their own boot-straps.

The second aspect of this emphasis on community involved the promotion of 'localism', with a new Act giving councils powers to buy out local facilities, such as swimming pools and libraries, faced with closure as a result of cuts to local authority spending. While the notion of 'community control' of facilities may seem attractive in the abstract, once again the reality is likely to be very different. First, there is the issue of funding; a proposed Big Society Bank, based on funds taken from unused bank accounts, will be unable to provide more than a fraction of the costs required to run these facilities; second, the proposal that local volunteers should replace skilled and qualified staff will be hampered not only by these volunteers' lack of skills but also by their lack of time, given that British workers already work among the longest hours in the European Community (Eurofund, 2009).

Opening up public services

The localism agenda is one element of wider public sector reform, with a Coalition White Paper entitled *Open Public Services* (dubbed the 'Big Society' Bill) published for consultation in July 2011 becoming the basis for the Public Services (Social Value) Act 2012. Its overarching aim is to open up *all* public services (other than the court system and the security services) to competition from 'any qualified provider'; outsourcing of services, in other words, will become the default position.

The belief that competition is the best guarantor of high-quality public services has underpinned the policies of both Conservative and New Labour governments since the late 1980s. However, as with the performance management regime discussed above, there is little evidence that the 'contract culture' which has developed as a result has led to an improved quality of care. On the contrary, as noted above, particularly within the third sector it has frequently led to a 'race to the bottom' with organisations vying to win contracts (Cunningham, 2008). As one experienced worker from a mental health voluntary organisation told us:

My experience has been that workers' conditions have gone down and down, the wages have gone down and down, the hours have gone up ... There is something about being professional in an organisation but how on earth do you provide empowering practice if workers are totally disempowered? I don't think it's possible. (Doreen, cited in Ferguson and Woodward, 2009, p 93)

Funding social care – 'shared responsibility'?

In February 2013, the Coalition Government committed itself to accepting the central recommendation of the Report of the Commission on Funding of Social Care and Support, chaired by Andrew Dilnot (Dilnot Commission, 2011), that individuals' lifetime contributions towards their social care costs – which are currently potentially unlimited – should be capped.

As a response to the crisis of social care in England, however (the only part of the UK to which the report applied), the Government's response is likely to prove utterly inadequate, for several reasons.

First, whereas Dilnot had recommended that the cap (the total amount which individuals are required to contribute towards the cost of their care) should be set at around £35,000, the government has set the figure at the absurdly high figure of £75,000. The result will be that millions of working-class people will still be required to sell their homes in order to fund residential care.

Second, as the author of a King's Fund report entitled *Beyond Dilnot* has argued, for most people the key issue is not protecting their savings. Rather:

The central challenge is to assess the total quantity of resources needed to ensure that people have access to the right level of support, currently limited in most places to people with substantial or critical needs. For many people it is eligibility for help, not protection from costs, that is the primary issue. This is especially the case for adults of working age with care and support needs arising from disability and chronic health conditions. (Humphries, 2013, p 3)

Third, while the notion of 'shared responsibility' for funding social care which underpinned the Dilnot proposals chimes with dominant notions of 'rights and responsibility', in a society where, according to an OECD study in 2011, the top 10% of people have incomes 12 times greater than the bottom 10%, up from eight times greater in 1985, and where the top marginal income tax rate dropped from 60% in the 1980s to 40% in the 2000s, there is clearly much more scope for a redistributive approach to the funding of social care than Dilnot envisaged (Ramesh, 2011).

Finally, as Peter Beresford and others have argued, a key contributory factor to the current crisis in social care was the division created in 1948 between a national health service, free at the point of use and funded out of general taxation, and a means-tested social care service, administered by local authorities. Part of the solution to the current crisis, then, Beresford has argued, is a national social care system based on the funding model of the NHS:

> The commission's recommendations will require substantial additional money from the public purse and Dilnot has been honest about this. But we might wonder why the commission hasn't gone the whole nine yards and argued for a free social care system funded from general taxation that can connect seamlessly with a universalist NHS. This is what most service users and members of the public appear to favour and is acknowledged to be the simplest and clearest funding model. (Beresford, 2011)

Conclusions: whither adult social work and social care?

As Lymbery has observed, there are strong parallels between the current transformation of social care and social work and the last major transformation of the 1990s which ushered in community care (Lymbery, 2010). Then as now, a new national system was rolled out on the basis of a very narrow (and selective) evidence base. Then as now, radical rhetoric ('the empowerment of users and carers') proved to be a smokescreen for privatisation, marketisation and the withdrawal of the state. And then as now, great claims were made for the liberating effect that the changes would have on both service users and practitioners (see eg Levick, 1992). As noted above, personalisation in particular has been presented as a way of 'liberating social work from the shackles of care management' or 'allowing social work to rediscover its mission' (Davies, 2012). The reality is proving to be very different, with more form-filling, increased bureaucracy and workers' judgement being questioned by funding panels.

Yet despite two decades of care management approaches and despite the failed promise of personalisation, all the evidence suggests that the overwhelming majority of social workers and social care workers remain committed to the welfare of those they work with and want to work in an empowering way. So how do we begin to begin to construct a welfare system based on people's needs and wishes, a genuinely 'popular social work'?

First, it must involve the building of new alliances and networks to overcome the divisions that both neoliberal and traditional welfare systems have created: professionals versus service users and carers, 'producers' versus 'consumers', professional social workers versus social care workers and so on. In truth, most of us are likely to be service users at some point in our lives, certainly of health services but often too of social care and social work services. Any progressive welfare system has to start from the shared experience of those who use services and those who work in them. In recent years, the Social Work Action Network in Britain has tried with some success to create a forum where these different groups can come together, debate ideas and agree on the form of collective united action, for example in relation to the defence of asylum seekers. Another example at local level is a personalisation network, initiated by UNISON activists in Glasgow, which has drawn together local authority social workers, staff from voluntary organisations, service users, carers and academics to challenge Glasgow City Council's cost-cutting model of personalisation.

Second, it means involvement in wider struggles against austerity and privatisation. Many social movements have a role to play in this but in our view the role of the trade union movement is central. This is not simply because with seven million members it remains by far the biggest collective movement in the country but also because of the potential economic power of its members. We saw a glimpse of that power on 30 November 2011 when more than two million workers, mainly from public sector workplaces, brought large swathes of the country to a halt in a strike in defence of pensions. Sadly, some trade union leaders, more concerned with letting off steam than with mounting a genuine challenge to the Coalition Government, called off that action almost immediately and an opportunity was lost. Given the current scale of the government's attacks on welfare, however, there will undoubtedly be opportunities for more sustained action in the coming period.

Third, it means learning from the *global* experience of welfare practitioners, activists and social movements, both past and present. In a series of publications in recent years, we have sought to excavate forms of popular social work that have often been 'hidden from history' (Lavalette and Ferguson, 2007) and also to make more widely known examples of radical practice from other countries, some of them a response to natural or man-made disasters (Ferguson et al, 2004; Lavalette and Ioakimidis, 2011).

Finally, the question of welfare cannot be divorced from the kind of society we live in. Many current forms of welfare would be unnecessary in a society with less poverty and inequality and where people had far greater control over their lives. Since 1999, two great social movements have challenged the neoliberal dominance of economy and society; the first, the anti-capitalist movement that emerged out of protests against the World Trade Organisation in Seattle in 1999 with its assertion that 'Another World is Possible', and more recently the Occupy Movement, whose slogan 'We are the 99%' found an echo with millions of people across the globe. In a world wracked by economic crisis and with the re-emergence in Europe of fascist parties which seek to shift the blame for that crisis onto the poor, the disabled and the refugees, involvement

—

by social workers and social care workers in such movements for radical social change is essential, both as a means of renewing and refreshing the profession and more importantly, as a contribution towards creating a society meeting human need rather than a market-driven 'race to the bottom' as the basis for social care provision.

Note

[1] In Scotland the history of the poor laws is slightly different. Historically, the poor law system was operated by the Church of Scotland ('the Kirk'). The 'Disruption' in the Kirk of 1843 split the Church of Scotland and brought turmoil to the system. A Royal Commission was set up in 1844, which led to the Poor Law Amendment Act 1845. Unlike the English and Welsh system the Scottish Act did not attempt to abolish outdoor relief. The workhouse, therefore, was an institutional home for the elderly and the disabled rather than an instrument of deterrence for the 'able-bodied poor'. These administrative differences did not make the plight of the Scottish poor any less taxing than their English and Welsh counterparts and, as the 19th century drew to a close, a more centralised Scottish system replicated, in the main, the system that operated through the rest of Britain.

The Big Society debate and the social care crisis

Bill Jordan

In July–August 2012, national euphoria around the success of the London Olympics proved that the UK is potentially a Big Society. A huge army of volunteers made millions of overseas visitors welcome all over the land; others supplied security and assistance at the Games venues themselves; citizens greeted each other in the streets and on public transport as fraternal comrades; and the whole nation united in celebration of the dedication and achievement of a small group of our fellow countrymen and women.

This proved that the idea of the Big Society, first canvassed by David Cameron (2009) in the lead-up to the 2010 general election, is not purely wishful thinking. People will help each other, volunteers will co-operate effectively with organised groups, big businesses and public services, and the experience of this will improve national well-being. But all this will only happen under very specific conditions, and through very skilled overall direction.

The Olympics were not perfectly organised, and the failures were significant. The most notable was the collapse of a contract for security staff with the largest employer in the private sector, G4S. In the end, police and soldiers filled the gap, but not before the whole world had learned about the company's shameful efforts to cut corners in its recruitment programme (last-minute and utterly slipshod) in its attempt to make money from the prestigious contract. It was the decision to outsource what would traditionally be the province of our state defence and security services, in order to save public funds, and not any inadequacy in the co-ordination of volunteers and voluntary organisations, which let the whole show down.

All this parallels the history of the Coalition Government's attempt to operationalise its notion of the Big Society through public policy. Using the rationale of the fiscal deficit and the austerity imperative, the new regime has cut public services and increased contracting-out since it came to power.

Meanwhile, the crisis in social care rumbled on through the Olympics period. As the Winterbourne View defendants went on trial and new scandals in the sector filled the media, the government dithered about whether to accept the Dilnot Commission's recommendations on funding. It was trapped by its own austerity rhetoric, because any credible plan, however long postponed, would look expensive, and would involve paying for the care of people who had substantial savings before the onset of the conditions which gave rise to their needs.

Furthermore, the social care sector was primarily 'delivered' by firms (both large and small) reliant on profits for their continuance. They notoriously saved costs by paying low wages, skimping on training and supervision, and recruiting well-qualified foreign workers on exploitative terms. There was no scope for further privatisation, and little realistic prospect of adequate regulation and inspection.

So the chances of linking any funding plan to the Big Society programme, or to the rhetoric of saving public expenditure through outsourcing, were strictly limited. Because the sector was already in private hands, there was no way the government could lead an initiative to introduce voluntary collective participation in the care of older people, as in the Olympic Games; and no way of saving more money through privatisation.

Of course, none of this means that social care is beyond the reach of the spirit of the Olympics or the Big Society. On the contrary, most care work is done on an unpaid basis by spouses, partners and neighbours, or by formal or informal community groups. But it does mean that, for the time being, the leadership of the drive to co-ordinate this mass collective effort, and forge it into a social movement with political clout and mutual support, must remain outside the political realm, in civil society.

Certainly professionals in the public sector, such as social workers, can support and promote such campaigns, and should do so. This will help the main body of those carrying the burden of both caring and putting pressure on the government, and assist in keeping up morale.

But it still means that millions of people with care needs (like those of my household) must continue to pay for them, up to an unlimited amount, and for an unlimited time-span. This government can see little electoral gain in announcing a plan for social care before 2015, and the costs are likely to scare off the Labour Party also. The lessons of the Olympics will go unheeded by politicians, but hopefully not by the people. We went to Weymouth to watch the sailing on 8 August 2012, and saw thousands of disabled elderly spectators receiving assistance from volunteers, family, friends and each other.

Academic study of the care crisis can capture only a small part of this collective effort, but it may gather a momentum of its own, which will eventually demand the attention of researchers and policy makers.

How the market fails social care

Mark Lymbery

It would require a breathtaking combination of naivety and gullibility to deny the central point of Ferguson and Lavalette's argument: there is indeed a crisis in adult social care in the early years of the 21st century. As I am, I hope, neither naive nor gullible I would not wish to position myself as a crisis-denier – in fact I take the view that the crisis has been several decades in the making, and that successive governments have ducked or misrepresented the problem. From my analysis this is not a tale from which any political party emerges with credit.

Consequently, I don't wish to contend any of the core points of their argument: rather, I intend to expand upon four issues that typify the problems that beset adult social care. Each of these separate themes is given added force when placed in the political context outlined by Ferguson and Lavalette. The first section will examine the principles that have suffused the two major changes of the last 20 years – community care and personalisation – alongside the limited and flawed evidence that has attended their introduction. This will be placed into a financial context: indeed, I will argue that a failure to grasp the financial nettle is the single biggest failure of policy in relation to adult social care. Finally, I will address the matter of regulation – closely involved in the Winterbourne View and Southern Cross scandals, with a particular link to the previous section being that the proper financial consequences of effective regulation have never been grasped.

Principles

The first objective of the Community Care White Paper was '... to enable people to live in their own homes wherever feasible and

---

sensible ...' (DH, 1989, p 5). This is important for an understanding of how the policy came to be widely accepted. For many, the avoidance of any form of institutional care was paramount, a principle that appeared to be placed at the forefront of policy. However, its implementation did not accord to this ideal as the realities of finance – expanded below – took precedence. Subsequently, much rhetoric that accompanied proposals to change the nature of care services focused on the failure of community care to live up to its high ideals (see ODI, 2008). A discourse of 'failure' became normal in relation to adult social care; the presumption was that previous policy urgently needed to be replaced (HM Government, 2008), an approach that was typical of the 'epochalist' thinking that characterised the New Labour approach to policy-making (du Gay, 2003; Lymbery, 2010). Nowhere was there any recognition that this 'failure' was an inevitable consequence of funding choices. Rather, it was suggested that the system was flawed, and that professionals – who were presumed to have contributed to this failure (Needham, 2011) – must act in a radically different manner (which chimed with a strong critique from the disability movement: Harris and Roulstone, 2011). To ensure that people could develop a preventative approach to problems within their own lives, it was argued that the nature of services should be rebalanced by focusing on earlier intervention, to counter the reliance on services being made available only to people with high levels of need. This focus has been consistently emphasised in numerous succeeding documents (HM Government, 2007; ODI, 2008).

The themes of choice and control, first trailed in the Green Paper (DH, 2005), were central to this change, underpinning the policy that has subsequently emerged, labelled either as personalisation or self-directed support. A central point is that it should transfer the responsibility of managing services away from the state onto individual service users. Having explored this with certain groups of service user, the previous government was sufficiently impressed as to require all services to be 'transformed' in accordance with these principles (DH, 2008). The current Westminster government is wedded to exactly the same set of ideals (DH, 2010a).

—

It is important to recognise that personalisation has attracted significant support from the disability movement (see Glasby and Littlechild, 2009). However, as a number of writers have pointed out, there are conceptual fault-lines in the policy (Ferguson, 2007; Houston, 2010; Lymbery, 2010; Spicker, 2012); consequently it is no longer acceptable simply to discuss personalisation in glowing terms, without subjecting some of its key elements to close scrutiny. Personalisation is intended to enable the restoration of people's rights as citizens (Oliver and Sapey, 2006) and challenge the paternalism of state decision-making (Ellis, 2007). However, the evidence for its success and its appropriateness as a guiding principle for the reorganisation of services is questionable – and in this respect a similar problem is clearly being replayed as with community care in the 1980s.

Evidence

There are similarities in the use of evidence to support both the introduction of community care and personalisation. In both cases, claims were made for the universal applicability of policies that were originally framed in relation to relatively small fragments of the adult population. If we examine community care first, the initial evidence demonstrated that it was particularly successful in tightly drawn pilot studies, featuring service users with complex sets of circumstances, with the active management of their cases by a skilled practitioner (Challis and Davies, 1986). Indeed, it was subsequently asserted that the case management role should be regarded as more complex than that of a social worker and should therefore be reserved for the most experienced and qualified staff members (Challis et al, 1995). The service response known as 'care management' was introduced on a universal scale despite the fact that evidence for its success came from only a few tightly controlled pilot projects (Bauld et al, 2000; Means et al, 2003).

If we turn to personalisation, a similar pattern can be observed – the policy once again is being introduced in the absence of robust evidence (Spicker, 2012). For example, while the evaluation of individual budget pilots was broadly positive, there were major concerns in relation to older people and people with cognitive impairments (Glendinning *et al*, 2008). Most of the articles to have emerged have focused on the potential of individual budgets rather than their limitations or weaknesses (see, for example, Rabiee et al, 2009), with relatively few commenting on the uneven levels of success (Netten et al, 2011). In addition, much was made of the potential of self-directed support to generate both improved outcomes and reduced costs (Leadbeater et al, 2008). However, the evidence base for this assertion was small, and does not convincingly reinforce the claims made on its behalf. Once again, therefore, the available research evidence cannot carry the burden of expectation that policy-makers have placed upon it – a point made trenchantly by Clements (2008) in relation to personalisation, but which also holds in relation to community care (Bauld et al, 2000). As I have previously observed, the government is repeating a basic error (Lymbery, 2010).

Finances

Lewis and Glennerster (1996) have convincingly argued that financial issues were paramount in the introduction of community care. The policy was needed because of the unintended consequences of the changes in supplementary benefit regulations in 1980, which had resulted in the state financially supporting people who entered residential or nursing home care, irrespective of need (Means et al, 2003). Because there was no way of controlling this budget it escalated hugely through the 1980s.

Consequently, a key purpose of community care policy was to curb expenditure, which was managed through the simple mechanism of transferring cash-limited budgets to local authorities (Lewis and Glennerster, 1996). This has been labelled the 'deep normative core' of community care (Lewis and Glennerster, 1996), and it subsequently overwhelmed the core principles of the policy. One action that linked financial control to the political motivations of community care was the requirement that 85% of the Special Transitional Grant (STG) – which amounted to £1,568m over the first three years of implementation – had to be spent in the independent sector (Lewis and Glennerster, 1996). This was both a clear indication of the government's priorities, and also provided 'cover' for the government to enable it to assert that the policy had been adequately funded (Lymbery, 2005).

The contrast between the government's approach then and now is stark. Despite well-publicised attempts to highlight the essential problems with funding and supporting long-term care (Sutherland, 1999; Dilnot Commission, 2011), successive governments have failed to establish ways of resolving these knotty problems. Certainly, it is now widely accepted that the financial settlement for adult social care is inadequate to the tasks confronting it (Dilnot Commission, 2011). However, there seems to have been a peculiar form of intransigence within government that fails to recognise the extent of this problem and which asserts – contrary to the evidence – that the settlement for adult social care is both fair and reasonable (DH, 2012a).

The austerity programme to which the Coalition Government is committed represents a major problem in this respect, despite little evidence that it will successfully achieve the goals that have been laid out for it (Taylor-Gooby, 2012). A word about the particularly traumatic financial environment is critical here. The New Labour government pledged to find £52bn in cuts – which was more than doubled by the incoming coalition, with a particularly harsh spending review in late 2010 indicating how these cuts were to be made (HM Treasury, 2010). A number of points must be made in relation to this:

- such swingeing levels of austerity have never been attained anywhere, not just in this country (Taylor-Gooby, 2012);
- the austerity measures disproportionately reduce spending as opposed to increasing tax (Taylor-Gooby and Stoker, 2011);
- local government is experiencing a particular burden – a reduction of 27% in their total budgets by 2014/15 (HM Treasury, 2010) – which is problematic as local government is largely responsible for the funding and delivery of adult social care (Glasby, 2011).

It is startling that local authorities are expected to bring about massive changes in their policies and practices at a time of such financial stringency. At the same time, the government has failed to bring forward concrete plans to resolve the problem the funding of long-term care, despite the fact that it has been estimated that there will be a 40% increase in expenditure between 2009 and 2029 if there is no change to current arrangements (Dilnot Commission, 2011), simply because of demographic change. The Funding Progress Report (DH, 2012b) appears to accept most of Dilnot's conclusions but states that there is no prospect of funding any changes until the next spending review, and that – even then – the decisions will be taken in the light of other priorities. As Ferguson and Lavalette have pointed out in the lead essay, it is not that such changes are unaffordable – rather that they don't represent a political priority.

The final point on funding relates to the clear contradiction between the principles of prevention and early intervention and the continuing requirements of eligibility criteria (Henwood and Hudson, 2008), noted earlier. It is clear that there was inadequate resourcing in social care even before the financial crisis of 2008 that ushered in the subsequent austerity programmes (CSCI, 2008); however, this conclusion was ignored when the revised criteria were published (DH, 2010b). Since the policy of personalisation was initially intended to reconcile the conflicting imperatives of cost control and early intervention, this failure has catastrophic consequences which appear to be unrecognised. As a result, many authorities continue to tighten up their eligibility criteria even though such action has been specifically warned against by government (DH, 2010a). Given that personalisation is heavily dependent on the principles of prevention and early intervention it is hard to see how this can be achieved in conditions of austerity.

Regulation

The problems of regulation – alluded to by Ferguson and Lavalette in their lead essay – also are long-standing. *Caring for people* (DH,

—

1989) created a requirement that local authorities acted to develop the independent sector, functioning as enablers and purchasers of care services rather than as the major providers. Lewis and Glennerster (1996) identified this as a 'near-core' activity, which was profoundly ideological in its nature. It hinged on a belief that the independent sector could bring the benefits of flexibility and efficiency to the provision of care, while maintaining higher standards of quality. In reality, as highlighted by recent events such as the abuse at Winterbourne View and the collapse of Southern Cross, the quality of independent sector care cannot be guaranteed and there are inadequate mechanisms to compel such quality. Indeed, the Serious Case Review into events at Winterbourne View (Flynn, 2012) explicitly notes that light touch regulation did not work and castigates Castlebeck Ltd (the private sector owners of the hospital) for being more concerned with profit than care quality. Similar criticisms can be levelled at the private equity form who asset-stripped Southern Cross, rendering their business model deeply problematic. Indeed, Scourfield (2012) has suggested that the reliance on private markets to provide care both is fundamentally flawed in principle and has highlighted the weaknesses of regulatory systems.

This is not to romanticise past practice in the public sector – there are numerous examples of inadequacies and abuse that could be cited. However, the fact that the majority of social care is now provided by the private sector creates specific problems. In particular, it is hard to account for public funds when care is provided by the private sector and there are major flaws in the systems of regulation that have been devised (Kerrison and Pollock, 2001), clearly evidenced at Winterbourne View (Flynn, 2012). Since the 'deep normative core' of community care was to save money – a principle that continues – there were never likely to be adequate systems for monitoring and inspection, as these would be very costly as well as difficult to manage. Because systems of trust and confidence simply cannot be applied in such circumstances (Harrison and Smith, 2004) the effectiveness of external regulatory systems is critical – but the emphasis has long been on the establishment of 'light touch' regulatory systems, where their effectiveness is much less certain (Bevan, 2008) in general terms, and completely inappropriate in principle in relation to social care.

Conclusion

Scourfield (2007) reminds us that the reason why the public sector first emerged was to ensure that people who required support could have it provided in a secure and dignified manner, being neither reliant on the quirks of the family or the vagaries of the market. The typical user of adult social care is not the fully autonomous rational being envisaged in the rhetoric of personalisation (Houston, 2010). Ways of resolving the crisis in adult social care need to start from this recognition. I am appalled that the commodification of social care continues apace: surely the message that we should learn from recent experiences is that social care is one example of an issue that is too important to be left to the market? In all cases the existence of appropriately skilled and professionally qualified workers to enable people to come to grips with a complex and apparently often heartless system will be essential. There is nothing about the direction of policy that gives me confidence that either point will come to fruition.

The crisis in social care: deepening the analysis

Dexter Whitfield

I agree with the thrust of the Ferguson/Lavalette analysis of the crisis in adult social care. This response proposes a clearer theoretical framework, challenges the use of some terms and suggests how the way forward can be developed.

Ferguson and Lavalette's article addresses the personalisation, marketisation and privatisation of public services, but does not fully address financialisation, despite it having a key influence on the way neoliberal care policies are designed and implemented. The capitalisation of income streams and securitisation of assets helped to commodify services and assets and extend markets and had a significant role in causing the 2008 financial crisis. A theoretical framework would help to fully understand the scope and scale of the commercialisation of social care and commodification of risk in Britain, and to make valid comparisons with other countries, particularly since public housing and social care were in the forefront of the drive to privatise the welfare state.

Financialisation, personalisation, marketisation and privatisation of public services are four sequential overlapping functions that have a central role in the implementation of neoliberal policies to reduce to role of the welfare state in a capitalist economy. Outright privatisation of many public services is not immediately possible economically or politically feasible, so new pathways had to be created to facilitate the mutation of privatisation via the marketisation of services by outsourcing, joint ventures, public–private partnerships, transfers to arm's-length companies and 'commissioning' of services to spur further competition (Whitfield, 2012a).

This was aided by fragmentation of the public sector into separate business units, trusts and companies, under the guise of increasing user choice and creating a diversity of service providers, but in practice designed to destabilise current provision and increase organisational change and outsourcing. Other key objectives included the transfer of risk and responsibility to individuals, driving down the cost of employment and imposing an austere financial climate by deep cuts in public spending by adopting a rapid deficit reduction strategy.

The mainstreaming of individual budgets, direct payments and vouchers issued to service users who are given a budget or direct payment to spend on defined services instead of being provided with services by the state, new and increased care charges, payment-by-results in which contractors and investors depend on performance-related contracts and profits, in parallel with the growth of a social investment market in bonds and shares, are other examples of the financialisation of health and social care.

So are the transfer of ownership and management of public facilities to community organisations under the guise of 'community asset ownership' and private finance initiative (PFI) and public–private partnership (PPP) projects that enable construction companies and banks to finance the design, construction and operation of public buildings, creating new markets and opportunities to extract profits?

Roots of the care crisis

A more in-depth analysis is required to identify the roots of the care crisis in the 1980–2000 period, as this was a key determinant of the current crisis. The privatisation of care homes, rampant outsourcing of home care, weak regulations, inadequate contract monitoring and the private equity strategy of separating care home ownership and operation using the sale-and-leaseback model were widely adopted. Unprecedented state financial support for private provision is also rooted in this period. There were early warnings of the pending crisis. *Cashing in on care* mapped out social needs and priorities and forecast the potential consequences of outsourcing and privatisation nearly three decades ago (NUPE/SCAT, 1984).

Ferguson and Lavalette correctly 'locate the roots of the current crisis in the market fundamentalist (or neoliberal) policies initiated by the Conservative governments of the 1980s, which for the most part were continued by New Labour governments from 1997 onwards'. Thus the reference to 'shock doctrine' overlooks the degree to which the marketisation and privatisation of social care were under way before the financial crisis, so it is not comparable with the radical policy changes usually associated with this concept. Spending cuts deepened the crisis and accelerated opportunities to further embed existing neoliberal social care policies.

It is also necessary to understand why the outsourcing and privatisation of social care proceeded much faster than in other public services. For example, many local authorities and private/voluntary sector care companies were able to evade the European Union staff transfer regulations by outsourcing through individual rather than block contracts. An individual care package does not constitute an 'economic entity' under the European Acquired Rights Directive. This ensured that private sector terms and conditions were the norm, allowing the social care market to grow rapidly, and helped to slow down public sector social care wage demands. In addition, many local authorities turned a blind eye to trusts and companies that cut jobs, and terms and conditions after the transfer or sale of care homes (for example, UNISON Essex County Council Branch, 2007 and UNISON North West Region, 1999).

Another element of this crisis was the slow approach taken by local authorities to improve and reconfigure social care provision. The belief in 'if it is working, don't fix it' led to significant differences in the quality of public provision within and between local authorities, reflecting good and bad management and variable distribution of resources. Social care improvement and innovation were fragmented, with trade unions responding primarily to budget cuts to protect jobs and services.

The reference to a 'public service industry' is misleading, because this is a flawed concept. It is not an economic definition because it is limited to 'all private and third sector enterprises that provide services to the public on behalf of government or to the government itself' (Julius, 2008). The term excludes privatised services such as water, transport, energy and telecoms, which are regarded as private services, so the 'industry' bizarrely gets smaller as more services are fully privatised! It also excludes in-house providers simply because they are in the public sector. The term implies there is a separate public sector industry, when in fact managed services companies and consultancies operate in larger private service markets. It is a UK-only definition, with limited application internationally. Targeting private companies conveniently deflects political responsibility.

'Corporate welfare' is a more appropriate term to fully understand the power and influence of transnational companies, trade and business organisations, allied with state interests in promoting deregulation, marketisation and privatisation (Whitfield, 2012b).

It is questionable whether 'Big Society' is an overarching framework for the Coalition's welfare policies. Despite the rhetoric, the term remains vague and was valuable to the Coalition primarily because they could present it as a 'new' or alternative policy. In practice, it is little more than an umbrella under which a ragbag of policies can be made to appear more coherent than they actually are.

The promotion of voluntary and social enterprises is a diversion to try to make commissioning, contestability and outsourcing politically acceptable. Transnational and large national companies dominate outsourcing and will continue to do so. Choice mechanisms encourage individual, not collective, decision-making and participation in markets and acceptance of the ideology of market forces. Community participation is viewed in a one-dimensional perspective, in which class, community, political, economic and other interests are ignored or marginalised (Whitfield, 2012b).

Extending alternative strategies

Ferguson and Lavalette concentrate on the key struggles needed to begin to construct a welfare system based on people's needs and priorities, such as new alliances and networks, the central role of the trade union movement, learning from radical practice in other countries and involvement in movements for radical social change. It is also imperative that we have a clearer perspective of a socialist model of social care, a prerequisite to mobilise community and trade union action and to build political support. Critical analysis of policies and exposing the failure of privatisation and private sector profiteering is rarely adequate.

A three-part reconstruction strategy is required for the economy, the state and public services (Whitfield, 2012b). This includes a range of economic and industrial policies, financial and regulatory reforms, clarity about the core functions of the state, intergenerational responsibilities and radical changes in public spending priorities. The degree to which neoliberal ideology and policies are embedded in political economy means that policies or regulations alone have limited effect.

The Ferguson/Lavalette strategy should be extended in five key ways. First, a radical reassessment of social care, underpinned by public service principles and values, could establish new strategies and policies that set out who delivers services, comprehensive regulatory frameworks, rigorous monitoring, inspection and scrutiny, and the development of new models of care. The re-municipalisation of outsourced and privatised services, for example, care homes, social work practices and the termination of PFI/PPP projects, should be accompanied by increased public investment in new housing and care options. However, there can be no return to existing managerial and operational practice, as this will only repeat the earlier failures.

Second, the future finance of social care must be addressed. The range and quality of social care options are increasingly linked to cashing-in housing assets, thus restricting the options available to those in the public and private rented sectors. The dramatic fall in house prices and the aggressive debt-fuelled takeovers of care home companies also exposed the flaws in this approach. All moves towards an asset-based welfare state model must be vigorously opposed.

—

The Dilnot Commission on Funding of Care and Support recommended a capping of lifetime contributions to adult social care costs after which costs would be eligible for full support from the state. The Commission had 'extensive discussions' with the financial services sector as the proposals would '... create a new space for financial products' linked to pensions, housing assets and insurance. Private equity and venture firms will be eager to develop new products. A cost-sharing model instead of fully funded state provision will exacerbate the current problems and increase the financialisation of social care.

Third, a new public service management should be developed to reverse the separation of client–contractor functions inherent in the commissioning model and recommit to in-house provision and improvement. The new approach should radically improve democratic accountability, social justice, and the quality of jobs and safeguard the public interest. The new public management (NPM) model must be replaced as it is fundamentally flawed because of its reliance on outsourcing and privatisation.

Fourth, a public infrastructure investment strategy is essential to create fully integrated and accessible health, housing, education and transport services and community facilities. The private finance of health and social care facilities via PFI and PPP projects fragments and marketises provision and is a costly and inflexible method of financing public infrastructure (Whitfield, 2010).

Finally, social care must be an integral part of the democratisation and consolidation of the public sector to transform governance and accountability and include service user, community organisation, staff and trade union involvement in the design, planning and delivery of care services. New disclosure and transparency regulations will be needed to ensure evidence-based policy-making and evaluation become a reality.

Challenging the market *and* the state

Ian Hood

Without a doubt people with disabilities are facing the greatest level of attack to their lives that we have ever seen. As the current government seeks to make major cuts in spending in all parts of the welfare state, people with disabilities face cuts in the income they receive through welfare benefits and in the support they need. Glibly the government talks of cuts of up to 20% in the payment of some benefits such as Disability Living Allowance and reductions of 14% in Housing Benefit from those who have committed the crime of having a spare bedroom in their house.

There seems to be no conception amongst those who make such decisions that there is a cumulative effect of these cuts. And on top of this, most people with disabilities are also facing exactly the same attacks that are hitting the rest of the population – wage freezes, health service reorganisation, job losses and cuts in a whole range of public services from library closures to cuts to the refuse collection.

At the heart of all we do is how we build the biggest alliance to challenge this approach. People with disabilities are part of the community both in their own lives and in their relations with others.

But I have concerns with the concept of 'marketisation'. The process that has taken place is not the same as the privatisation of the NHS or of other public services. The level of private sector involvement in the provision of care for people with disabilities is much smaller than in elderly care sectors. The voluntary sector is the major provider of services and the 'four legs good, two legs bad' approach to state provision of social care is problematic.

The authors of the lead essay rightly note the long roots of discrimination and marginalisation of people with disabilities that

—

began with the rise of capitalism. This is particularly important for people with learning disabilities who were particularly affected by this as their traditional occupations became mechanised and requiring greater skills levels.

However later in their analysis they see a particular attack on the welfare state of the post-war period by the politics of Labour and the Tories in the 1980s and 1990s. The problem with this is that it supports an argument that there was some genuine transformation in the welfare state in the period of the 1940s and 1950s which we should look back to as an example.

We would disagree with this. It was the post-war period that saw the biggest rise in numbers of people resident in learning disability hospitals. Thousands more were incarcerated in huge hospitals for no reason as part of this great growth in the welfare state. We have no interest in going back.

'Marketisation' is an inadequate term to explain what has been going on. Very little of the social care provision provided by local authorities has been transferred to the voluntary or the private sector. Even during the well-deserved closures of the long-stay hospitals most staff were retained within the NHS, if they chose to stay. The purple line in Figure 1 below shows a very small fall in residual NHS expenditure over the last 15 years.

A similar process took place with the few hostels run by local authorities which were reprovisioned. Most staff were transferred within the local authority sector. No local authority day centres in Scotland we know of have been transferred, while, of course, some have been shut.

It is the intense growth in spending on social care services over the last 15 years that has transformed the situation and led to the huge growth in multimillion pound voluntary organisations.

Figure 1 shows the spending in Scotland on learning disability services since 1996. The orange line shows the inflation rate over the same period. The red line shows that it is the voluntary and private sector that have grown fastest over this period – an almost eightfold growth in funding. It is this growth in additional spending which led to

—

the growing importance of the voluntary sector. But it is important to note that the gap between the dark blue (total local authority spending) and the red line has doubled in the 15-year period, indicating that local authorities are spending more than ever on their own services. In the early days of community care, the relationship between local authorities and the voluntary sector was similar to that of other grant givers. Voluntary organisations had broad latitude to deliver support and services based on shared values. The Griffiths reforms of the early 1990s were about bringing this relationship under the control of the state.

Figure 1: Learning disability spending in Scotland, 1996–2010

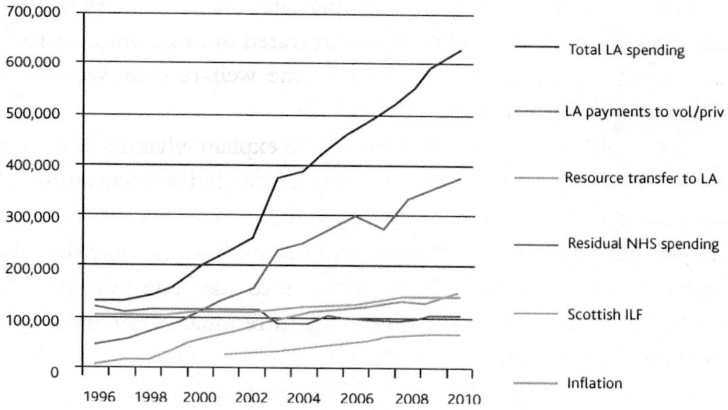

Source: Based on figures from the Scottish Government

The growth of payments to the voluntary sector over the last 15 years is not linked to a growing independence of the voluntary sector. Instead, most of this additional income is tied to a growth in contract culture which constrains what voluntary sector providers can do. The reality of relations between the voluntary sector and local authorities is more one sided than the phrase 'marketisation' implies. There has been a growing dependence of voluntary sector providers on the blessing of local authority commissioning staff.

The relationship is more similar to that of arm's length external organisations (ALEOs) that have grown from local councils hiving off their own departments but often without the network of personal relationships that gives former staff influence over council decisions.

As a result the voluntary sector has all the disadvantage of being externalised with none of the advantages. Therefore we see situations like those in Glasgow over the last few years where the local council has first imposed cuts of 15% on voluntary providers then followed this by a further 20% reduction through the introduction of individual budgets to service users. Organisations have been told to get on with it and that the council have no responsibility for what they pay their staff.

This attack here is driven by local authorities. The process referred to as 'marketisation' is more of a process where the state tries to take control of these large budgets in the hands of the voluntary sector and to determine how and why this money is spent.

Our choice cannot be either the rule of the free market or the return to the days of 'state planning' in some kind of Gosplan monolith. We need to reject the 'state planning good, marketisation bad' model.

Instead we have been working with people with learning disabilities to help them make their own space to determine their own lives. In so doing we are willing to challenge all those who would take control of their lives — whether it is the state in capitalist society or private companies (whatever their organisational form).

For people with learning disabilities it is the local state that they often have to challenge. In 2009 when Edinburgh City Council tried to tender out support services, the people who used these services claimed ownership and demonstrated and protested until the council caved in. The process of production line 'personalisation' by Glasgow City Council has been and remains under challenge from those who have been subject to it. In Aberdeen and Dundee, attempts by local councils to close day centres and to 'modernise' by forcing people out of them into inadequate community facilities have been challenged.

People with learning disabilities themselves have been at the heart of this process, partly to defend the services that they value irrespective of whether it is the state or the voluntary sector that provides them, but also to reclaim a sense of who they are within this society.

For a short while in Paris in 1968, education was transformed into a new paradigm: one in which it was education of equals. Lecturers and students were no longer placed in a formal hierarchy but debated ideas together. Lecturers brought additional knowledge but interpretation and understanding was shared and developed jointly.

People with learning disabilities are fighting to create a social work of equals where they contribute on a par with others. Social work professionals or social care staff may bring particular knowledge but its use and application should come from a shared understanding. We have a long way to go in this journey but it has begun. But it cannot be done by looking back to the myth of the welfare state; instead, we must go forward – together.

Personalisation: the experience in Glasgow

Brian Smith

Ferguson and Lavalette's contention that the current UK Coalition Government is intent on using the present crisis of capitalism to drive through massive attacks on how social care is provided is well made. The fact that the Labour Party and, in Scotland, the SNP are not doing more to resist these significant structural changes in how care is organised and provided is likely to lead to further conflicts between local councils and their social care workforces, service users, carers and communities. The drive towards more privatisation of public services, cuts in social care support for the most vulnerable and reductions in the social care workforce's wages and employment conditions, particularly by voluntary organisations, corporate charities and profit-making private companies, have to be fought.

As the authors point out, Glasgow City Council's decision to use the policy of personalisation (self-directed support) as the primary means of achieving spending cuts in the city's social care budget undermines any notion of individual empowerment and choice for the vast majority of the city's 4,000 citizens who receive support through the adult social care services budget (the policy is being rolled out to children with a disability in 2013 and to those over 65 years old after that). Glasgow City Council aims to cut 20% from its total spending on current adult care service users over the two years from 2012 to 2014. The council has defended this by saying that 9% of this will be redirected to new service users not currently in receipt of any support. However, that still means that 11%, or £10m from the total 2012 budget of £90m, is being cut from adult social care in the city over two years. The council says that managing a smaller cake means that some people must get less in order that others get something – the question of course is: will

—

anyone get what they really need to ensure basic care never mind deliver social participation? A recent UNISON survey of workers in the city's adult care teams confirmed the disconnection between the council's promotion of individual budgets as 'helping you do things you want to do' with the senior management's messages to frontline staff that the individual budgets simply need to cover life-and-limb risks. The main choice many people in Glasgow may have to face in the future could be around how many hours of basic care their individual budget can buy them – considerations about the quality of that service or the wages and employment rights of those who provide it may just not feature. Such a situation benefits no one except those wishing to make disabled people and those who work in social care pay for the mistakes of big business bosses and their bankers. The trade union's survey concluded that staff do not have the resources to implement the policy properly and this is leading to a slump in morale, not to mention the obvious impact on service users and their families. The use of personalisation by Glasgow City Council to cut spending is leading to job losses and wage cuts in the city's charity sector as many organisations attempt to 'stay in the social care market' by cutting the unit costs of the care they offer. Fewer workers, of course, means fewer services, and cuts in wages and staff training will only lead to a less confident and stable social care workforce. Cherry-picking of the most profitable areas by the private sector will undermine quality and co-ordination of services. The 'race to the bottom' will also see the remaining services that are provided directly by the council's workforce come under pressure unless this step-up in the marketisation of care in the city is resisted.

In early 2011, UNISON activists working in both the council and some charity organisations agreed that a campaign against the council's budget cuts through personalisation was necessary. The campaign built on the Defend Glasgow Services Campaign launched by the UNISON Glasgow City Branch in early 2010 to resist planned cuts by the then UK Labour Government. The Defend Glasgow Services Campaign continues to call on the council to stand up to both the current UK and Scottish Governments by refusing to make any cuts by setting budgets that protect current services, while leading a fight

—

to win more money for the city. A lobby of the council in April 2011 on the potential impact of personalisation was attended by 400 people, including many disabled people and carers who were not involved in any campaign groups but were fearful of what may be coming. This led to a network being established involving service users, carers, UNISON, Learning Disability Scotland, SWAN, Carers Coalition Scotland and Black Triangle. The network meets every six weeks or so and has organised several more protests, a well-attended conference and a hustings meeting during the 2012 Scottish Council elections. The network has challenged the council's needs assessment scheme for allocating individual budgets, assisted service users and carers to access advocacy and representation, linked people up with legal advisors and gained some significant local media coverage. While the council has not as yet shifted from its overall public position of aiming to make the two-year £10m cut in adult social care, most involved in the campaign feel that we have helped hold off some of the cuts. The campaign continues.

The Scottish Government intends to roll out self-directed support across Scotland in the coming months and has said that the policy must not be a cover for cuts. However, if other local councils adopt the Glasgow approach then that is exactly what it will be. UNISON Scotland remains concerned about the possible impact on services and the social care workforce and also intends to deploy additional trade union resources around the recruitment and organising of personal assistants employed through individual budgets.

The UK Government's attack on welfare benefits and its lack of a real job creation programme represent further attacks on the most disadvantaged. Disabled people should have the opportunity to access decently paid, permanent employment with proper support arrangements funded by the employer. However, what disabled people face at the moment are cuts in their current benefit entitlements and a chronic lack of job opportunities. Those in work face poorer employer support arrangements and increasingly aggressive absence management procedures which often breach even the limited employment rights that UK disabled workers can assert in what is the most deregulated labour

—

market in Europe. How many of the UK's inspirational paralympics athletes will face cuts in their benefits or no job in 2013?

Ferguson and Lavalette are correct to point out that some of the policy frameworks and service provision in Scotland are not as market-driven as in England. Free personal care for older people, a resistance to privatisation in NHS Scotland and free NHS prescriptions are to be welcomed. However, both the Scottish Government and local councils are making the overall level of cuts in public spending asked of them by the UK Government. This is having a huge impact on the provision of adult social care with thousands of jobs in council social work departments and support organisations lost in recent years and the introduction or increase in charges for living aids, home adaptations, home care, community meals, and so on. Cordia, the arm's-length council company that provides the majority of home care in Glasgow, has reduced contact time for service users, cut workers' unsocial working pay enhancements, intends to cut 500 jobs in 2013 and wants to discuss with the trade unions the idea of not paying the Scottish public sector living wage of £7.20 per hour to new workers or when bidding for new work. A campaign to defend home care services and those who provide them is likely to be required.

The Scottish Government is also proposing to integrate aspects of the budgets of the NHS and local councils, particularly in the area of older people's care. They intend to do this by way of primary legislation in the coming year. This is to be done to 'gain efficiencies'; however, at this stage it appears to be more about implementing the UK Government's austerity programme. The Scottish Government claims that it can free up monies from current NHS acute ward spending, move cash into community care services and thus reduce 'delayed hospital discharge' (which they used to call 'bed blocking') and also maintain people in their home for longer before hospital care is required. There is nothing wrong with these aims but the Scottish Government has failed to say where the money in the NHS will be released from or how councils are expected to move from a situation where they are aggressively cutting community care services to one where provision is expanded to a level which would make a significant impact in delaying a person's entry into hospital. It is also ironic that in Glasgow, where a three-year experiment in merging social work and health management structures and some budgets fell apart in 2010, figures for delayed discharge are now among the best in the country. This is likely to be due to decent joint working between health and social work staff at the coalface and perhaps shows that top-down mergers are often an expensive distraction when trying to improve services for real people. There are also issues about how current social care budgets would be democratically controlled if removed from local councils.

UNISON has also spent a significant amount of time in recent years at both Scottish and local levels raising with social care employers the need for proper staff supervision arrangements that are supportive, offer access to quality training and enhance individual practice development. The need for robust workload management schemes that protect workers from overwork, work-related stress and work-related absences are also crucial. The social care workforce is not to blame for the cuts or the fall-out of the economic crisis and the trade unions must do all they can, including the use of industrial action where necessary, to defend their members from the pressures of unacceptable work demands.

As Ferguson and Lavalette point out, past advances in the provision of welfare and care were won via working-class pressure and the future will be no different. Solidarity between social care workforces, service users, carers and wider communities will be crucial in the fight against the profit-driven economic system of the 1%, and the trade unions must play a central role in that fight and the anti-cuts movement.

Background information

UNISON Glasgow City Branch has 11,000 members across the city council, its companies, ALEOs and in the city's seven FE Colleges. The UNISON membership in the city's Social Work Services Department is 3,500, which is over 80% of the workforce.

Supporting informal carers

Claire Cairns

On 1 October 2012 over 150 carers filled the Scottish Parliament in the UK's first ever Carers' Parliament. Carers, who are the heart of the care system, were briefly at the centre of Scottish politics, with their voices replacing those of our elected representatives.

For many it was an opportunity to celebrate how far we have come in recognising the immense contribution carers make to our communities. Certainly over the last few years politicians from all parties have been vocal in their support of carers, keen to recognise their 'sacrifices' and their role as 'unsung heroes'.

On the surface things are moving in the right direction for carers. Emerging health and social care policy is littered with references to how important it is to support carers, to consult with them and recognise their role as contributors to care provision. There is also no doubt that there have been improvements in the support carers can access, not least through the development of the network of carer centres, which can now be found in almost every local area.

But how do carers themselves view the current care system and the transformational changes planned for it? And if it is in crisis, how is it affecting them?

Many of the carers who spoke in the debate acknowledged that the policy was often right, but they were badly let down by the systems and processes that seem determined to keep them from the accessing the support they need. One carer talked about her eight-year struggle to get a diagnosis for her son, another about the eight months it took to get a shower seat; others spoke about giving up their jobs, then seeing their savings eroded due to loss of income and the additional costs related to caring. One carer simply said: 'What I require is sleep

– respite a few nights a week, but not every area offers this.' Another spoke of needing an operation, but of having to discharge herself from hospital because nobody was there to pick up the care at home.

Carers don't want to be 'unsung heroes'. They want prompt access to quality services for the people they look after, they want to be able to get a break for themselves when they need it, they want the same training and safeguards that paid workers enjoy.

More than anything carers want rights. There is still no statutory duty to support carers. They have the right to an assessment, but no right to services they are assessed as needing. While this remains the case, whatever the policy says, carers are at the whim of local authority budgets. When hard decisions are made and budgets are cut, local politicians will prioritise the services they are legally required to provide.

Yet supporting carers is not just a moral imperative. There are also compelling financial arguments for protecting carers' health by ensuring they have access to support at an early stage of their caring role. To put it simply, the cost of small and inexpensive interventions at the right time is far less expensive than providing full-time replacement care when a carer becomes ill, or the caring relationship breaks down due to carer strain.

The Princess Royal Trust for Carers calculated that an investment of less than £5 million in carer support services resulted in at least £73 million worth of social gains in a year.[1] This gain in value arises from carers maintaining better physical and mental health by reducing stress and depression. In addition to this, the person who is cared for is more likely to be able to continue living at home, while carers are more likely to be able to remain in employment.

There is a strong argument for viewing carers as an essential and finite resource which requires protection and investment, much the same as the health and social care workforce is viewed, particularly since all the plans to reshape health and social care services are reliant on shifting the balance of care from the acute sector to more care at home and in the community. For these plans to succeed they will require the

—

cooperation of carers. Without their contribution of unpaid care the desired savings will not be achievable.

So why is the system so often failing to deliver on its promises, failing to provide carers with the support they need and the people they care for with the personalised preventative services so often described as the way forward? Why is transformational policy being stalled or undermined by poor systems and practice?

To answer this question we need to recognise that policy and systems often work against each other, with high ambitions being undercut by the reality of spending cuts, increasing demands and the reluctance of the workforce to embrace change.

First, we know that preventative services play a key role in preventing crisis and enabling people to better self-manage long-term conditions. They help to avoid costly hospital admissions and can prevent or delay the need for residential and nursing care. However, the shrinking budget for social care has resulted in a growing gap between demand and resources, and the response from local authorities is to balance this by the tightening of eligibility criteria. As a result, people struggle even to get an assessment, never mind a service. It requires patience, persistence and know-how to navigate your way through the system and many people drop out, only to re-emerge when they are at a crisis point.

Second, the introduction of personalisation and self-directed support as a mechanism to deliver better outcomes and better value for care services is reliant on service providers having the freedom and ability to develop a range of innovative, quality services for people to choose from. Yet increasingly local authorities are using the tendering process to force service providers to cut costs to the bare minimum, often with the loss of what made the service both unique and personal in the first place.

In November 2011 the Coalition of Care and Support Providers Scotland (CCPS) collected information about hourly rates by issuing a Freedom of Information (FOI) request to all Scottish local authorities, seeking disclosure of the rates paid to external providers for care and support, and the equivalent cost of council in-house services.[2] According to the returns submitted, at least 50 care services throughout Scotland are being funded by councils at a rate of less than £10 per hour: these costs include staff salaries and related employer costs; training, qualifications and workforce development; regulatory and compliance fees; and organisational overheads. The highest costs were generally found to relate to council's own in-house care services, with several of these costing up to 100% more than the most expensive externally provided service of the same type. According to similar data which were gathered in 2007, ten of the 30 councils that responded have lowered their hourly rates over the last four years.

CCPS also looked at the impact hourly rates had on the quality of care provision by examining them against the quality gradings produced by the Care Commission. They demonstrate that the voluntary sector has the best overall track record for quality of care and support at home compared with the private sector and council in-house provision, with a significantly greater proportion of gradings at '5' and '6' ('very good' and 'excellent') for housing support and care at home services.

This FOI exercise tells us that hourly rates paid to the voluntary sector are, in general, higher than those paid to the private sector, but lower than the cost of in-house provision. Linking this to the gradings information published by the regulator, it seems reasonable to conclude that whilst high cost does not automatically translate into high quality, there may be a price point at which low hourly rates mitigate against the successful delivery of support that is deemed 'very good' and 'excellent'.

If the voluntary sector is forced to compete in a market which values cost reduction above quality, then what will this mean for the successful implementation of personalisation? We are told that self-directed support will help to open up this marketplace, by directing resources towards the services that people most value, but how will this be achieved when at best recipients will have the same budget as the council to purchase services and in many cases they will be allocated a much lower amount?

In conclusion, emerging policy poses both opportunities and threats to carers and the people they care for. If the balance of care shifts,

—

without a corresponding shift of resources to support people to stay at home, the burden on unpaid carers will undoubtedly increase.

Cuts must not be allowed to fall disproportionately on the most vulnerable members of our society. This is not the time to disinvest in social care, when we are going through a period of upheaval and transformation with a view to redesigning services to meet the challenges of our changing demography. At the same time more emphasis needs to be placed on the quality of services, rather than allowing social care procurement practices, driven by costs, to initiate a race to the bottom.

Furthermore it is not just a question of resources – systems and processes are equally important. They should be about empowering people, not preventing people from accessing support for as long as possible. We need to foster true co-production, with carers and service users being treated as equal partners and having a guaranteed place at the strategic planning groups where the real decisions are made. This, after all, is what personalisation is meant to be about, placing the users of services at the heart of their design.

Notes

[1] The Princess Royal Trust for Carers Social Impact Evaluation Report, Baker Tilly, March 2011.

[2] 'Hourly rates for care and support', Report into a Freedom of Information Exercise by CCPS, June 2012.

Some concluding remarks

Iain Ferguson and Michael Lavalette

Mark Lymbery starts his response to our lead article by noting that:

> It would require a breathtaking combination of naivety and gullibility to deny the central point of Ferguson and Lavalette's argument: there is indeed a crisis in adult social care in the early years of the 21st century.

Each of our respondents has added flesh to our assertion and each has enriched the argument by making clear the depth of the crisis we now face. This is particularly powerful given the range of backgrounds each comes from.

The contributions by Claire Cairns and Brian Smith remind us that, whilst the precise details of adult social care practices differ across the different UK jurisdictions, the cuts are exposing a huge gap between the policy rhetoric and the reality as implemented through practice. The two Glasgow case studies provide detailed coverage of the impact of the cuts on social care budgets on the front-line and of their impact on workers, service users and carers. For these reasons alone, the contributions from both respondents will resonate with people across the UK – and, indeed, across much of the Eurozone where austerity measures are being implemented and front-line services being left exposed and underfunded.

As Smith declares, we need to oppose a logic which argues that 'some people must get less, in order that others will get something'. This is a position which finds us all scrambling and fighting against each other for a few meagre crumbs, when the reality is that, even in these so-called austere times, the cake is big enough to feed all those in need: the Sunday Times Rich List for 2012 showed that, despite the crisis, the wealthiest 1,000 people in Britain have seen their wealth soar to record levels and now stands at a combined total of £414.260 billion (http://www.therichest.com/rich-list/nation/sunday-times-rich-list/).

Mark Lymbery adds important reflection and detail to our case. He starts with the moves towards community care in the late 1980s. His point that the rhetoric of the community care policy initiatives was able to gain wide support because it embodied an implicit critique of the existing paternalistic provision, often situated in large, depersonalised institutions, is well made. It is a point that also resonates with some of the themes raised by Ian Hood. Of course, the reality of the community care policy as it was rolled out, and the financial restrictions that ran alongside it, meant that it failed to achieve what many service users and carers expected or wanted. The framing of community care as 'policy failure', Lymbery suggests, laid the basis for the turn towards personalisation.

Lymbery traces the trajectory of personalisation 'policy formation' and suggests it is remarkably similar to that which produced the community care legislation. He suggests that the personalisation policy agenda has been built upon a partial reading of the causes of the adult social care crisis, a critique of professionalism (which resonates with politicians but also with many people within the service user movements), utilisation of small pilot projects to 'showcase' the project but with little evidence to support the policy turn, and with financial restrictions tied into the policy, which has also been implemented against a backdrop of austerity and cuts. Thus the rhetoric of the policy and the hopes it engendered within some sections of the service user movements are likely to be dashed.

—

The two most critical contributions come from Dexter Whitfield and Ian Hood. Whitfield takes us to task for not having a clear understanding of the relevance of 'financialisation' within the present crisis and for utilising Klein's (2008) concept of 'shock doctrine'. He doesn't give a definition of 'financialisation' but essentially this is a concept that refers to the ways that finance, over the last 30 years, has grown on a massive scale to play an unprecedented role within the capitalist system. Chris Harman gives some of the detail:

> The stock market valuation of US financial companies was 29 percent of the value of non-financials in 2004, a fourfold increase over the previous 25 years; the ratio of financial corporations' to non-financial corporations' profits had risen from about 6 percent in the early 1950s through the early 1960s to around 26 percent in 2001; global financial assets were equal to 316 percent of annual world output in 2005, as against only 109 percent in 1980; household debt in the US was 127 percent of total personal income in 2006 as against only 36 percent in 1952, around 60 percent in the late 1960s and 100 percent in 2000. (Harman, 2009, p 278)

We perhaps did not emphasise these longer, deeper trends within capitalism enough here – although we have done so elsewhere (Ferguson and Lavalette, 2013) – but Whitfield is correct to argue that the present crisis of care is a direct result of decisions taken over the last 25–30 years that have seen British governments become some of the leading advocates of neoliberal policy regimes in the world. These decisions have opened public service provision up to forms of 'corporate welfare' that have allowed some companies to make vast profits from the public purse.

The various ways in which the market has encroached into public service delivery – full privatisation, outsourcing, internal marketisation, the use of 'arm's length' companies, the competitive and regulatory pressures placed upon the voluntary sector to effectively force it to adopt 'business models', and so on – have opened up vast divisions in care provision, have made some people exceptionally wealthy, have undermined the pay and conditions of front-line workers, and have had a negative impact, by and large, on services and the needs of service users and carers. Although Whitfield doesn't mention it here, it has also had a negative impact on any notion of democratic accountability. Prior to the early 1980s councils and councillors weren't bastions of democratic engagement, but at least there were mechanisms in place that provided some degree of accountability over the provision of services such as schools, housing and social services. One of the less spoken about consequences of the spread of 'corporate welfare' has been the creation of a 'democratic deficit', where working-class people have no democratic means of holding service providers to account.

So we agree with much of Whitfield's analysis. But we would like to emphasis the political context within which these developments took place. Whitfield rightly points out the various ways in which public services were effectively subjected to privatising pressures. He notes that a full-frontal privatisation in the 1980s was not possible. This was partially a consequence of the heightened atmosphere of class conflict that marked the 1980s and early 1990s. The Thatcher Governments of the 1980s were particularly focused in their attempt to deal with the trade unions, but were determined to take the more powerful unions on one at a time – they were fearful of provoking a generalised trade union response to their policies (for a development of this argument, see Lavalette and Mooney, 2000). Over the same period a number of Labour councils (Sheffield, London, Liverpool) tried to defend council services in the face of national government dictate. By the time Thatcher got elected for the third time (in 1987) the opposition had suffered significant defeats (in the mines, docks and newspapers industries and in each of the 'opposition' councils); 1987 became the 'social policy watershed' year with general election commitments to significant welfare reform in the NHS, social services and schools and through the introduction of the community charge (poll tax).

The response of the Labour Party to all this was very significant. Under the leadership of Neil Kinnock, Labour followed what they termed the 'dented shield' policy. For Kinnock and the Labour

—

leadership this meant that the job of Labour councils was not to challenge Conservative government policies, but to implement policies efficiently and to maintain levels of service provision – concern over who provided such services, and an 'ideological opposition' to privatisation were, at best, secondary considerations. Thus the basis of bipartisan political commitments to 'outsourcing', to arm's length companies, to methods of new public management, to the private finance initiative and so on were laid. As Lymbery notes: 'this is not a tale from which any political party emerges with credit'.

Whitfield ends his contribution by outlining the need for an extended 'socialist strategy' for public and care services. This is an important point of departure. For too long those of us on the Left and the radical Left have not paid enough attention to the vision of another world that we all assert is possible. Part of Whitfield's solution is to reconstitute some of the forms of state delivery that marked the 'pre-neoliberal' era. We are sure, if he had had the space, that he would have added various caveats about 'democratic control', and about who has the right to assert what their services should look like. This is something that Hood makes clear in his contribution. Hood is dismissive of the 'welfare moment' and argues that too many of us paint too rosy a picture of the realities of welfare provision under the 'classic' social welfare state.

Hood is correct to emphasise some of the negative aspects of the post-war welfare state. It was full of assumptions about women's role in society, about families, about sexuality, about disability (and the domination of medical models) and about 'race' and who should get access to services. Welfare professionals at various levels were given priority over decisions about the 'best interests' of 'clients', thus it embodied professional authority and hierarchy and it created vast bureaucracies (which was part of the Left's critique of welfare long before it was adopted by the political right). No one wants to return to this.

Yet our analysis is one-sided if we concentrate only on these aspects of state welfare. If we recognise only the oppression and inequality within state-provided services then when a hospital or school is

—

privatised surely we should celebrate the removal of an 'oppressive institution'! But, of course, we campaign to defend the school and the hospital, not because we don't recognise their failings, but because we recognise that under capitalism state-provided services, free at the point of use, can mitigate, to some extent, the iniquities of naked market capitalism.

Thus, whilst Whitfield is in danger of glorifying state welfare in the past, Hood is in danger of ignoring the gains that were associated with some aspects of state welfare provision. There is, of course, a contradiction here – but the contradiction is embedded in the nature of capitalism and the shifting, contradictory and conflictual ways that welfare operates within the confines of capitalism itself.

These are issue that need a full airing – but this is not the appropriate place. The crisis of adult social care requires analysis and political action. We need to deal with the immediate requirements of adults with a range of needs and we need to be clear that full and effective care, free at the point of use and shaped by the needs of service users and carers, is possible and affordable in modern Britain. The alternative, of abandoning people to the market, of unequal treatment depending on wealth and income, of residual care for the poor, would be a marker of the degradation of public life in Britain and a reminder of the continuing relevance of Marx's claim that 'Capital ... takes no account of the health and the length of life of the worker, unless society forces it to do so' (Marx, 1867/1976).

References

Bauld, L., Chesterman, J., Davies, B., Judge, K. and Mangalore, R. (2000) *Caring for older people: an assessment of community care in the 1990s*, Aldershot, Ashgate.

BBC (2012) 'Budget 2012: George Osborne cuts 50p top tax rate', available at: www.bbc.co.uk/news/uk-politics-17450719

Beresford, P. (2010) 'An opportunity to reconnect with social work's values', *Community Care – The Big Picture*, available at: http://www.communitycare.co.uk/blogs/social-care-the-big-picture/2010/10/by-peter-beresfordin-a-sea.html

Bevan, G. (2008) 'Changing paradigms of governance and regulation of quality of healthcare in England', *Health, Risk & Society*, vol 10, no 1, pp 85-101.

Borsay, A. (2004) *Disability and social policy in Britain since 1750: a history of exclusion,* London: Macmillan.

Bowers, T. (2012) 'Guy Hands' Terra Firma poised to buy Four Seasons care homes', *The Guardian*, 29 April.

Callinicos, A. and Simons, M. (1985) *The Great Strike: the miners' strike of 1984–85 and its lessons*, London: Socialist Worker.

Cameron, D. (2009) Speech on the Big Society, Hugo Young Memorial Lecture, IPPR, London, 9 November.

Campbell, J. and Oliver, M. (1996) *Disability politics: understanding our past, changing our future*, London: Routledge.

Challis, D. and Davies, B. (1986) *Case management in community care*, Aldershot, Gower.

Challis, D., Darton, R., Johnson, L., Stone, M. and Traske, D. (1995) *Care management and health care of older people*, Aldershot, Arena.

Charlton, J. (2000) 'Class struggle and the origins of stayte welfare reform', in M. Lavalette and G. Mooney (eds) *Class struggle and social welfare*, London: Routledge.

Clements, L. (2008) 'Individual Budgets and irrational exuberance', *Community Care Law Reports*, vol 11, September, pp 413–30.

Community Care (2013a) 'Nationwide care threshold "will exclude hundreds of thousands in need"', available at: www.communitycare. co.uk/articles/28/06/2013/119290/nationwide-care-threshold-will-exclude-hundreds-of-thousands-in-need.htm

Community Care (2013b) 'State of Personalisation 2013', available at: www.communitycare.co.uk/state-of-personalisation-2013

Conservative Party home page (2010) 'Cameron unveils "Big Society' Plan"', 31 March, available at: http://www.conservatives.com/ News/News_stories/2010/03/Plans_announced_to_help_ build_a_Big_Society.aspx

Coote, A. (2011) 'Big Society and the New Austerity' in M.Stott (ed) *The Big Society challenge*, Norfolk: Keystone Development Trust Publications, pp 82–93.

CQC (Care Quality Commission) (2012) *Learning disability services inspection services: national overview*, available at: http://www.cqc.org. uk/sites/default/files/media/documents/cqc_ld_review_national_ overview.pdf

CSCI (Commission for Social Care Inspection) (2008) *Cutting the cake fairly: CSCI review of eligibility criteria for adult social care*, London, CSCI.

Cunningham, I. (2008) 'A race to the bottom? Exploring variations in employment conditions in the voluntary sector', *Public Administration*, vol 86, no 4, pp 1033–53, available at: http://dx.doi. org/10.1111/j.1467-9299.2008.00752.x

Cunningham, I. and Nickson, D. (2011) 'Empowering who? Personalisation and its implications for work and employment in the voluntary sector', Paper presented at International Labour Process Conference, Dublin, Ireland.

Davies, N. (1998) *Dark heart: the shocking truth about hidden Britain*, London:Vintage.

Davies, O. (2012) 'White Paper should allow social work to rediscover its mission', *The Guardian*, 8 March, www.guardian.co.uk/social-care-network/2012/mar/08/white-paper-social-work-mission

DH (Department of Health) (1989) *Caring for people: Community care in the next decade and beyond*, Cm 849, London, HMSO.

—

DH (2005) *Independence, well-being and choice*, London, The Stationery Office.

DH (2008) *Moving forward: using the learning from the individual pilot projects*, London: DH.

DH (2010a) *A vision for adult social care: capable communities and active citizens*, London, DH.

DH (2010b) *Prioritising need in the context of Putting People First: a whole system approach to eligibility for social care – Guidance on eligibility criteria for adult social care, England*, London: DH.

DH (2012a) *Caring for our future: reforming care and support*, Cm 8378, London, DH.

DH (2012b) *Caring for our future: Progress report on funding reform*, Cm 8381, London, DH.

Dilnot Commission (2011) *Fairer care funding: the report of the Commission on Funding of Care and Support*, London, HM Government.

du Gay, P. (2003) 'The tyranny of the epochal: change, epochalism and organizational reform', *Organization*, vol 10, no 4, pp 663–84.

EHRC (Equality and Human Rights Commission) (2011) *Close to home: an inquiry into older people and human rights in home care*, London: EHRC.

Ellis, K. (2007) 'Direct payments and social work practice: the significance of "street-level bureaucracy" in determining eligibility', *British Journal of Social Work*, vol 37, no 3, pp 405–22.

Emmanuel, R. (2009) Interview, available at: www.youtube.com/watch?v=1yeA_kHHLow

Engels, F. (1845) *The condition of the working class in England*, available at: https://www.marxists.org/archive/marx/works/1845/condition-working-class/index.htm

Englander, D. (1998) *Poverty and Poor Law reform in 19th century Britain 1834–1914,* London: Longman.

Eurofund (2009) *Working conditions in the European Union: working time and intensity,* Luxemburg: European Fund for the Improvement of Living and Working Conditions, available at: www.eurofound.europa.eu/pubdocs/2009/27/en/1/EF0927EN.pdf

Ferguson, I. (2007) 'Increasing user choice or privatizing risk? The antinomies of personalisation', *British Journal of Social Work*, vol 37, no 3, pp 387–403.

Ferguson, I. (2008) *Reclaiming social work: challenging neoliberalism and promoting social justice*, London: Sage.

Ferguson, I. (2011) 'The return of fear', *International Socialism Journal*, vol 130, available at: www.isj.org.uk/index.php4?id=719&issue=130

Ferguson, I. and Lavalette, M. (2013) 'Critical and radical social work: an introduction', *Critical and Radical Social Work: an international journal*, vol 1, no 1, pp 3–14.

Ferguson, I. and Woodward, R. (2009) *Radical social work in practice*, Bristol: Policy Press.

Ferguson, I., Lavalette, M. and Whitmore, E. (eds) (2004) *Globalisation, global justice and social work*, London: Routledge.

Flynn, M. (2012) *Winterbourne View: a Serious Case Review*, South Gloucestershire Safeguarding Adults Board.

Francis, R. (2013) *Independent Inquiry into care provided by Mid Staffordshire NHS Foundation Trust January 2005–March 2009* (the Francis Report), London: The Stationery Office, available at: http://www.midstaffspublicinquiry.com/report

Garganas, P. (2012) 'Interview – Greece: the struggle radicalises', *International Socialism Journal*, vol 134, available at: www.isj.org.uk/index.php4?id=793&issue=134

German, L. (1989) *Sex, class and socialism*, London: Bookmarks.

Glasby, J. (2011) 'Adult social care', in N. Yeates, T. Haux, R. Jawed and M. Kilkey (eds) *In defence of welfare*, Social Policy Association, available at: www.social-policy.org.uk

Glasby, J. and Littlechild, R. (2009) *Direct payments and personal budgets: Putting personalisation into practice*, 2nd edn, Bristol: Policy Press.

Glendinning, C., Challis, D., Fernandez, J.-L., Jacobs, S., Jones, K., Knapp, M., Manthorpe, J., Moran, N., Netten, A., Stevens, M. and Wilberforce, M. (2008) *Evaluation of the individual budgets pilot programme: final report*, York, Social Policy Research Unit, University of York.

Gilbert, Sir M. (2009) *Churchill and eugenics*, The Churchill Centre, available at: www.winstonchurchill.org/support/the-churchill-centre/publications/finest-hour-online/594-churchill-and-eugenics

Goffman, E. (1961) *Asylums*, London: Penguin.

Goodman, D. (1998) *No thanks to Lloyd George: how the old age pension was won, the forgotten story*, London: Third Age Press.

Gosling, P. (2008/2011) *The rise of the 'public services industry'*, updated 2011, London: UNISON.

Gough, I. (1979) *The political economy of the welfare state*, London: Macmillan.

Griffiths, R. (1988) *Community care: agenda for action* (the Griffiths Report), London: HMSO.

Harman, C. (2009) *Zombie capitalism*, London: Bookmarks.

Harris, J. (2003) *The social work business*, London: Routledge.

Harris, J. and Roulstone, A. (2011) *Disability, policy and professional practice*, London, Sage.

Harris, J. and White, V. (eds) (2009) *Modernising social work: critical considerations*, Bristol: Policy Press.

Harrison, S. and Smith, C. (2004) 'Trust and moral motivation: redundant resources in health and social care?', *Policy & Politics*, vol 32, no 3, pp 371–86.

Harvey, D. (2005) *A brief history of neoliberalism*, Oxford: Oxford University Press.

Henwood, M. and Hudson, B. (2008) *Lost in the system? The impact of fair access to care*, London: Commission for Social Care Inspection.

HM Government (2007) *Putting people first*, London, HM Government.

HM Government (2008) *The case for change: why England needs a new care and support system*, London: Department of Health.

HM Treasury (2010) *Spending Review 2010*, Cm 7942, London, The Stationery Office.

Hobsbawm, E. (1987) *The age of empire 1875–1914*, London: Abacus.

Holman, B. (2011) 'Big Society, Big Con?', Speech at the 6th Social Work Action Network Conference, University of Birmingham, 15 April.

Houston, S. (2010) 'Beyond *Homo Economicus*: recognition and self-realization and social work', *British Journal of Social Work*, vol 40, no 3, pp 841–57.

Humphries, J. (1977a) 'Class struggle and the persistence of the working class family', *Cambridge Journal of Economics*, vol 1, no 3, pp 22–49.

Humphries, J. (1977b) 'The working class family, women's liberation and class struggle: the case of nineteenth century British history', *Review of Radical Political Economy*, vol 9, pp 11–23.

Humphries, R. (2013) *Paying for social care: beyond Dilnot*, London: King's Fund, available at: www.kingsfund.org.uk/blog/2013/05/beyond-dilnot-need-wider-reform

Jones, C. (2005) 'The neo-liberal assault: voices from the frontline of British social work' in I. Ferguson, M. Lavalette and E. Whitmore (eds) *Globalisation, global justice and social work*, London: Routledge

Jones, K. (2000) *The making of social policy in Britain 1830–1990*, London: Athlone.

Jordan, B. (2011) 'Making sense of the "Big Society": social work and the moral order', *Journal of Social Work*, published online, 6 May, available at: http://jsw.sagepub.com/content/early/2011/05/05/1468017310394241

Julius, D. (2008) *Public Services Industry Review*, for Department for Business Enterprise and Regulatory Reform, London, available at: www.bis.gov.uk/files/file46965.pdf

Kane, D. and Allen, J. (2011) *Counting the cuts: the impact of spending cuts on the UK voluntary and community sector*, London: National Council for Voluntary Organisations.

Kerrison, S. and Pollock, A. (2001) 'Caring for older people in the private sector in England', *British Medical Journal*, vol 323, no 7312, pp 566–9.

Kimber, C. (2011) 'The welfare stakes', *Socialist Review*, April, available at: www.socialistreview.org.uk/article.php?articlenumber=11618, accessed 3/5/12

Kirkup, J. (2011) 'World facing worst financial crisis in history, Bank of England Governor says', *Telegraph*, 6 October, www.telegraph.co.uk/finance/financialcrisis/8812260/World-facing-worst-financial-crisis-in-history-Bank-of-England-Governor-says.html

Klein, N. (2008) *The shock doctrine: the rise of disaster capitalism*, London: Penguin.

Langan, M. and Schwarz, W. (1985) *Crises in the British state 1880–1930*, London: Hutchinson.

Lapavitsas, C., Kaltenbrunner, A., Labrinidis, G., Lindo, D., Meadway, J., Michell, J., Painceira, J.P., Pires, E., Powell, J., Stenfors, A., Teles, N. and Vatikiotis, L. (2012) *Crisis in the Eurozone*, London: Verso.

Lavalette, M. and Ferguson, I. (eds) (2007) *International social work and the radical tradition*, Birmingham: Venture Press.

Lavalette, M. and Ioakimidis, V. (eds) (2011) *Social work in extremis: Lessons for social work internationally*, Bristol: Policy Press.

Lavalette, M. and Mooney, G. (2000) '"No Poll Tax here": the Tories, social policy and the great Poll Tax Rebellion 1987–1991', in M. Lavalette and G. Mooney (eds) *Class struggle and social welfare*, London: Routledge.

Leadbeater, C., Bartlett, J. and Gallagher, N. (2008) *Making it personal*, London: Demos.

Levick, P. (1992) 'The Janus face of community care legislation: An opportunity for radical opportunities', *Critical Social Policy*, vol 12, pp 76–81.

Lewis, J. and Glennerster, H. (1996) *Implementing the new community care*, Buckingham, Open University Press.

Lymbery, M. (2005) *Social work with older people: context, policy and practice*, London, Sage.

Lymbery, M. (2010) 'A new vision for adult social care? Continuities and change in the care of older people', *Critical Social Policy*, vol 30, no 1, pp 5–26.

Marx, K. (1867/1976) *Capital*, vol 1, London: Penguin.

Mason, P. (2009) *Meltdown: the end of the age of greed*, 2nd edn, London: Verso.

Means, R., Richards, S. and Smith, R. (2003) *Community care: policy and practice*, 3rd edn, Basingstoke, Palgrave.

Mooney, G. and Scott, J. (eds) (2012) *Social justice and social policy in Scotland*, Bristol: Policy Press.

Morris, N. (2012) 'Crisis in care of elderly as £1bn cuts bite', *The Independent,* 18 April.

NUPE (National Union of Public Employees) and SCAT (Services to Community Action and Trade Unions) (1984) *Cashing in on care*, London, available at: www.european-services-strategy.org.uk/publications/archive/cashing-in-on-care-national-union-of-public-em/

Needham, C. (2011) *Personalising public services: understanding the personalisation narrative*, Bristol, Policy Press.

Netten, A., Jones, K., Knapp, M., Fernandez, J.-L., Challis, D., Glendinning, C., Jacobs, S., Manthorpe, J., Moran, N., Stevens, M. and Wilberforce, M. (2011) 'Personalisation through individual budgets: does it work and for whom?', *British Journal of Social Work*, advance access doi:10.1093/bjsw/bcr159

O'Connor, S. and O'Muchu, C. (2011) 'Britain's private care faces crisis', *Financial Times*, 30 May.

ODI (Office for Disability Issues) (2008) *Independent living: a cross-government strategy about independent living for disabled people*, London, ODI.

Oliver, M. and Sapey, B. (2006) *Social work with disabled people*, 3rd edn, Basingstoke, Palgrave.

Phillipson, C. (1982) *Capitalism and the construction of old age,* London: Macmillan.

Public Accounts Committee (2012) *The Care Quality Commission: regulating the quality and safety of health and adult social care*, London: HMSO.

Rabiee, P., Moran, N. and Glendinning, C. (2009) 'Individual budgets: lessons from early users' experiences', *British Journal of Social Work*, vol 39, no 5, pp 918–35.

—

Ramesh, R. (2011) 'Income inequality growing faster in UK than any other rich country, says OECD', *The Guardian*, 5 December, available at: www.guardian.co.uk/society/2011/dec/05/income-inequality-growing-faster-uk

Ridley, N. (1988) *The local right: enabling not providing*, London: Centre for Policy Studies.

Scourfield, P. (2007) 'Social care and the modern citizen: client, consumer, service user, manager and entrepreneur', *British Journal of Social Work*, vol 37, no 1, pp 107–22.

Scourfield, P. (2012) 'Caretelization revisited and the lessons of Southern Cross', *Critical Social Policy* vol 32, no 1, pp 137–48.

SCWIS (Social Care and Social Work Improvement Scotland) (2011) *Glasgow City Council Scrutiny Report*, April, SCWIS.

Slorach, R. (2011) 'Marxism and disability', *International Socialism*, vol 129, pp 111–36.

Spicker, P. (2012) 'Personalisation falls short', *British Journal of Social Work*, doi: 10.1093/bjsw/bcs063.

Stedman-Jones, G. (1984) *Outcast London*, 2nd edn, Oxford: Clarendon.

Sutherland, S. (1999) *With respect to old age: Long term care – rights and responsibilities: a report by the Royal Commission on Long Term Care*, London, The Stationery Office.

Taylor-Gooby, P. (2012) 'Root and branch restructuring to achieve major cuts: the social policy programme of the 2010 UK Coalition Government', *Social Policy and Administration*, vol 46, no 1, pp 61–82.

Taylor-Gooby, P. and Stoker, G. (2011) 'The Coalition programme: a new vision for Britain or politics as usual?', *The Political Quarterly*, vol 82, no 1, pp 4–15.

Thomson, M. (1998) *The problem of mental deficiency: eugenics, democracy and social policy in Britain 1870–1959*, Oxford Historical Monographs.

Timmins, N. (1996) *The five giants: a biography of the welfare state*, London: Fontana.

Toynbee, P. (2010) 'The "big society" is a big fat lie – just follow the money', *The Guardian*, 6 August.

UNISON Essex County Council Branch (2007) *Does Excelcare really care? An investigation into the transfer of 10 residential care homes by Essex County Council to Excelcare Holdings PLC*, European Services Strategy Unit, available at: www.european-services-strategy.org. uk/outsourcing-ppp-library/transfers-and-externalisation/does-excelcare-really/essex-excelcare-report.pdf

UNISON North West Region (1999) *The future of Tameside Care Group*, European Services Strategy Unit, available at: www. european-services-strategy.org.uk/outsourcing-ppp-library/ transfers-and-externalisation/the-future-of-tameside-care-group/ tameside-care.pdf

Whitfield, D. (2010) *Global auction of public assets: public sector alternatives to the infrastructure market and public private partnerships*, Nottingham: Spokesman Books.

Whitfield, D. (2012a) *The mutation of privatisation: a critical assessment of new community and individual rights*, Research Report No 5, European Services Strategy Unit, available at: www.european-services-strategy. org.uk/news/2012/the-mutation-of-privatisation-a-critical-asses/

Whitfield, D. (2012b) *In place of austerity: reconstruction of the state, economy and public services*, Nottingham: Spokesman Books.

Wintour, P. and Stewart, H. (2013), 'Spending review: George Osborne targets benefits and slashes public sector jobs', *Guardian*, 27 June, www.guardian.co.uk/politics/2013/jun/26/george-osborne-spending-review-benefits.

Yeates, N., Haux, T., Jawad, R. and Kilkey, M. (eds) (2010) *In defence of welfare: the impact of the spending cuts*, London: Social Policy Association.